ADRIANA LUNA CARLOS
Editor-In-Chief, Designer
and Co-Founder

HANNA OLIVAS
Managing Editor
& Co-Founder

NICOLE CURTIS
Director of the SRS
Magazine Division

H.A.N.N.A.
MAGAZINE

**ADVERTISING
OPPORTUNITIES**
Info@SheRisesStudios.com

H.A.N.N.A. MAGAZINE
JANUARY 2025

SHE RISES
STUDIOS

CONTACT US
SheRisesStudios@gmail.com
www.SheRisesStudios.com

www.SheRisesStudios.com

LETTER FROM THE EDITORS

Dear Readers,

Welcome to the January 2025 edition of H.A.N.N.A Magazine, where we are proud to kick off the year with a new vision for the future. This edition brings to the forefront incredible voices and stories of resilience, strength, and transformation. As we step into 2025, we celebrate the unwavering spirit of those who have not only overcome adversity but are now using their experiences to help others. We are excited to introduce Traci Powell, the founder of The Rebuilt Woman, on our front cover. Her dedication to empowering high-achieving women and healthcare professionals grappling with PTSD, depression, and anxiety is truly inspiring. Traci's personal journey and the groundbreaking work she does in her private practice are featured in this month's cover article, showcasing her unique approach to healing and transformation.

As we embrace the theme of New Year, New Vision, we are reminded of the power of fresh starts and the limitless possibilities that come with each new year. It is a time to reflect on the past and set intentions for the future, recognizing that each new beginning offers an opportunity to transform and grow. The journey toward personal and professional renewal is a path that requires courage, self-reflection, and a commitment to creating positive change. Whether it's healing from past struggles or pursuing new goals, the new year serves as a reminder that no matter where we start, the potential for growth and transformation is always within reach. Embracing a new vision allows us to take bold steps toward a more fulfilling life, one filled with purpose, resilience, and renewed self-belief.

Additionally, we invite you to join us in Las Vegas on February 22, 2025, for EmpowerHer Content Day—a day dedicated to empowering voices, creating connections, and sparking meaningful change in the lives of women everywhere. You won't want to miss this transformative event, and we've included all the details inside this issue. We're also proud to spotlight Voices of Hope 2025, an initiative that showcases individuals making an extraordinary impact on the world, inspiring others to take action and effect change. The coming year is filled with hope, and we are thrilled to share these powerful narratives with our global audience.

We hope this issue sparks inspiration and encourages you to step into the new year with confidence, purpose, and a renewed sense of vision. As always, thank you for being a part of the H.A.N.N.A Magazine community. We look forward to continuing to amplify your voices and stories throughout 2025 and beyond.

Warm regards,

Adriana Luna Carlos and Hanna Olivas
Editors of H.A.N.N.A. Magazine

SHE RISES STUDIOS

FENIX TV

EMPOWER**HER** CONTENT DAY

at

Elevate Your Brand Through Creative And Impactful Content!

EmpowerHer Content Day equips attendees with the tools and knowledge needed to craft compelling content for social media, podcasts, and videos.

FEBRUARY 22, 2025

TOTAL ACCESS TICKET: $127

WWW.SHERISESSTUDIOS.COM

EMPOWERING HIGH-ACHIEVING WOMEN AND HEALTHCARE PROFESSIONALS TO OVERCOME PTSD, DEPRESSION, AND ANXIETY

Traci Powell's journey from a long-standing career in neonatal care to becoming a beacon of hope in mental health and trauma recovery is one of profound transformation and purpose. With decades of experience as a highly respected neonatal nurse practitioner, Powell embodied the roles of caregiver, single mother, and school volunteer. However, behind her success was a silent struggle that would ultimately inspire her to redefine her life and career. Today, through her practice, The Rebuilt Woman, Powell helps professional women heal from trauma and attachment wounds, empowering them to reclaim their lives.

Powell's transition began with her own personal reckoning. For over forty years, she carried an undercurrent of depression, one that sat persistently in her gut despite her outward positivity. Like many professionals in healthcare, she kept her struggles hidden, fearing judgment or questions about her competence. As her responsibilities mounted, so did the mental toll. Eventually, her brain and body could no longer suppress the weight of her experiences. Panic attacks became constant, and suicidal thoughts emerged, forcing her to confront the reality of her mental health.

"I spent years never telling anyone about what I had been through and believing there was something wrong with me because I couldn't 'let go of the past,'" Powell shares. "I had no choice but to deal with it."

She started with weekly therapy, a common path for many, but it left her feeling worse. Repeatedly revisiting the traumas of her past seemed to deepen the emotional wounds rather than heal them. Determined to free herself from the past, Powell embarked on a search for a more effective solution. She eventually discovered a practitioner offering three-day trauma healing intensives, a method that transformed her life. This experience became the catalyst for Powell's new mission: to help other women achieve the same freedom. She returned to school, earning her post-master's degree as a psychiatric mental health nurse practitioner (PMHNP), and launched The Rebuilt Woman to help professional women heal and move forward.

Powell's personal journey deeply influences her therapeutic approach. She learned firsthand that traditional trauma therapy often focuses solely on the traumatic events themselves—the abuse, accidents, or crises. However, what many fail to recognize, Powell explains, is the significance of attachment wounds: the absence of the emotional nurturing every child needs to thrive.

"There are two kinds of wounds we carry," she says. "Trauma wounds, caused by the bad things that happen to us, and attachment wounds, which result from the good things that should have happened but didn't."

For Powell, addressing attachment wounds was the key to lasting transformation. She describes how healing these wounds allowed her to move beyond the feelings of sadness, insecurity, and self-doubt that had controlled her for so long. Through her three-day intensive process, Powell takes a unique approach, combining ego state therapy —which nurtures the wounded inner child—and trauma resolution therapy to heal traumatic memories trapped in the brain. As a nurse practitioner, she also incorporates nervous system regulation, recognizing how trauma and attachment wounds dysregulate the body and contribute to physical symptoms, persistent anxiety, and sleep issues.

Her method is both holistic and practical, providing an accelerated path to healing. Instead of clients spending years in weekly therapy, Powell offers them the time, space, and guidance to address the root of their struggles. "When the root problem is healed, lasting relief happens," she explains.

The outcomes of The Rebuilt Woman's three-day intensives speak for themselves. Women arrive burdened by anxiety, depression, and frustration, often feeling hopeless and stuck. They leave with a renewed sense of self, empowered and calm, their faces often marked by a clarity and peace they thought impossible.

Powell describes the process as a journey of meeting the emotional and developmental needs of the wounded child within, helping clients reconnect to their authentic selves. "It's like treating an infection causing a fever. If you only focus on the symptom—the fever—it will return. You need to heal the root infection," she explains. By addressing the foundational wounds, Powell helps women achieve not just relief from symptoms, but true and lasting healing.

Many clients have shared that they finally understand the source of their struggles. Some express surprise at the realization that even without explicit abuse, growing up in emotionally neglectful environments left them with deep-seated feelings of unworthiness. Powell's intensive structure allows them to heal these wounds, release emotional blocks, and experience breakthroughs that would otherwise take years in traditional therapy.

Powell's comprehensive approach is bolstered by her training in hypnotherapy, neurolinguistic programming (NLP), and Eye Movement Desensitization and Reprocessing (EMDR). These methods enable her to work with the subconscious mind and nervous system to create lasting change. Powell has also developed her own process, combining Developmental Needs Meeting Strategy—an ego state therapy—with NLP and trauma memory resolution. This integrative approach targets both the mind and body, helping clients release emotional pain, rewire negative patterns, and achieve transformation.

Having been a healthcare professional herself, Powell understands the unique challenges faced by high-achieving women. Perfectionism, emotional suppression, and imposter syndrome are common themes among her clients, many of whom feel pressure to maintain an image of competence and composure.

"Many healthcare professionals hold themselves to impossible standards, and they're often afraid to admit they're struggling," Powell notes. "But the truth is, unresolved trauma and stress don't just go away. They show up in our bodies, our relationships, and our minds."

Through her practice, Powell provides a safe space for these women to heal. Her work helps them release the emotional weight of past experiences, reconnect with their authentic selves, and cultivate resilience.

Powell's commitment to mental health advocacy extends beyond her practice. Recognizing the emotional toll the nursing profession takes, she launched the Nurses Healing Nurses initiative, a private Facebook community offering support and resources to nurses experiencing toxic stress. "I saw how many nurses were silently struggling with PTSD, anxiety, and depression," she explains. "By telling my own story, I gave other nurses permission to share theirs."

The group provides a safe space for nurses to connect, share experiences, and find tools for healing. Many members have reported feeling more resilient, less burned out, and better equipped to manage the challenges of their profession and personal lives. The initiative is a testament to Powell's belief that no one should suffer in silence.

Through her contributions to The Rebuilt Woman, her work with Nurses Healing Nurses, and her own story of transformation, Traci Powell is a beacon of hope for women seeking to heal from trauma and rediscover themselves. Her message is clear: true healing is possible, and no one is beyond hope.

For those who have spent years carrying invisible wounds, Powell's work offers a powerful reminder that the past does not have to dictate the present. Through compassion, expertise, and her unwavering commitment, she continues to help women move forward—not just surviving, but thriving.

CONNECT WITH TRACI

www.facebook.com/TraciPowellNP
www.TheRebuiltWoman.com
www.linkedin.com/in/traci-powell-np

LOOKING BACK AT THE INEVITABLE

by Debra Hillard

Remembering Myself-A Journey Through the Threads of Time has been percolating for decades, long before my pen ever hit the page. What I could not know at the outset, was the depth and breadth of what would eventually reveal itself to be shared, not until it finally happened. That event changed the course of my life forever and my once nearly smothered embers, are now ablaze.

This is not a story in the usual sense. Though I write about my life, this is not a memoire or a linear recounting of events as they occurred. These are excerpts from a life that has woven in and out of time, usually with some degree of awareness that I was not living solely in what appeared to be my present. I am referring to the fact that my experience of living these last seven decades has taken me deep into other lifetimes, other realities, and back again to the physical reality of the 21st century. My experience continues to be one of operating in multiple dimensions at once, aware of parallel realities and timelines. My story, as with my experience of living, weaves through them as if they were all occurring simultaneously.

As a child I knew that I was here for a specific purpose. I knew who I was before I ever had the words to speak. It has taken decades for me to shed the identity I adapted to survive and to step into the truth of who I have always known myself to be. If you asked me as a child who I was, I automatically said *"I'm an artist."* Those were the only words I had to assign to a vision far beyond my comprehension. They were words I could hide behind, an identity others could accept.

Along the way, there were forks in the road, decisions that shaped the *"what"* of my life. The who was my constant, but I was indoctrinated into a belief system that made it almost impossible for me to live that to the fullest. For most of my life, I felt compelled to contort myself into someone others would find acceptable.

Had I shared my reality with anyone, my fear was that I would be cast out as crazy. My only hope of survival was in being something greater than I was expected to be, but not truly myself.

It was only in the process of revisiting my life that the pieces began to fall into place. The pain and heartbreak made sense in a way that they could not while I was in the thick of it all. Every twist and turn along the way, each choice I made when presented with a fork in the road, and multitudes of images and poetic musings, began to paint a masterpiece of a life guided by Spirit. Though maturity was required to grasp the immensity of the shift I share at the conclusion of the book, the journey itself has been my true masterpiece thus far. As an artist, I have always said that my life would be my greatest work of art and this has proven to be the case.

This is a book I had to write. Just like I made the choice to live it all, sharing it is now part of that process. It is in honor of all of us who make the impossible choice to do our soul's work, no matter the cost. My hope is that something within the pages of this book ignites the smoldering flame within you that has been waiting to be fanned.

CONNECT WITH DEBRA

www.facebook.com/dkhillardart
www.instagram.com/dkhillard
www.linkedin.com/in/debra-hillard-93526913
www.dkhillard.com
www.dkhillardart.com

FROM DOUBT TO ACTION: HOW I BUILT THE CONFIDENCE TO LAUNCH MY VISION

by Brianne Rush

For years, I wondered how I was meant to give back. My career had been fulfilling—I'd climbed the ladder in both journalism and marketing—but I felt a tug to do something more. I wanted to take my experiences and turn them into something meaningful, something that could help others navigate the challenges I once faced.

That's how *The Independence Lab* was born.

But putting myself out there didn't come easily. I worried about what people would think. Would they believe I had anything valuable to share? Could I really make a difference? These doubts echoed in my mind as I took the first steps to launch this new venture.

Despite the fear, I went for it.

The Independence Lab is my way of giving back to women who are navigating the tricky transition from college to career. I remember the anxiety of those early days all too well—the uncertainty of finding my place, the self-doubt about my abilities, and the overwhelming sense of starting from scratch. It wasn't easy, but I figured it out. And now, I want to share the lessons I learned along the way.

Taking the Leap into the Unknown

My career journey began when I moved to New York City before my college graduation to chase a dream of becoming a magazine editor. That leap was terrifying—I had no roadmap, no guarantee of success, and a mountain of uncertainty. But I took the chance, and it paid off.

I worked my way up quickly, starting as a fact-checker before earning the role of managing editor for *Dance Spirit* magazine. It was a dream realized, but the journey wasn't without its challenges. I learned to work long hours, juggle competing demands, and navigate the politics of a highly competitive industry.

When I transitioned into marketing, I had to push myself even further outside my comfort zone.

I took a role at Kuno Creative, a digital marketing agency, as its first content manager and built a new department from the ground up. From there, I grew into the role of VP of Operations, where I've helped shape the company's culture, processes, and growth strategy.

Through it all, I learned some of the most important lessons of my career—lessons that I now share through *The Independence Lab*.

Lessons From a Life of Bold Moves

If there's one thing my journey has taught me, it's this: the biggest growth comes when you're willing to embrace discomfort.

When I moved to New York, I had no idea how I'd adapt to a new city, a new job, and a new way of life. But I showed up every day, asked questions, and worked harder than I thought I could.

When I transitioned into marketing, I had to learn an entirely new skill set. I didn't know if I'd succeed, but I leaned into the challenge and figured it out as I went.

And when I stepped into sales—a role I never envisioned for myself—I had to confront my own fears head-on. I was nervous, unsure, and far outside my comfort zone. But I pushed through, and it turned out to be one of the most rewarding experiences of my career.

Here are a few key lessons I've learned along the way:

1. **Your comfort zone will never lead to greatness.** Growth requires risk. Whether it's taking on a new role, tackling a challenging project, or starting something entirely new, the path to success is rarely easy.
2. **Your impact is greater than you think.** I used to question whether I could truly help anyone. But every time I share my story or offer guidance, I see how much it resonates. You don't have to be perfect to make a difference—you just have to care.
3. **It's okay to be scared. Do it anyway.** Fear doesn't mean you're unqualified or incapable. It means you're stepping into something new, and that's where the magic happens.

Finding the Courage to Give Back

Starting *The Independence Lab* has been one of the most fulfilling things I've ever done. It's given me a platform to share the lessons I've learned, connect with women who are going through the same challenges I faced, and help them build the confidence they need to succeed.

If you're considering taking a bold step in 2025—whether it's starting a new venture, changing careers, or pursuing a passion project—know this: you are capable of more than you think. The doubts and fears will come, but they don't have to hold you back.

As we head into a new year, I challenge you to think about your own bold vision. What's the one thing you've been putting off because it feels too big, too scary, or too uncertain? Write it down. Say it out loud. Take the first step.

You don't have to have it all figured out. You just have to start.

CONNECT WITH BRIANNE

www.TheIndependenceLab.com

SHE RISES STUDIOS

WE WISH YOU A

Happy New Year

Wishing you a year filled with new **hopes**, new **dreams**, and new **achievements**.

www.SheRisesStudios.com   www.fenixtv.app

5 TIPS WHEN TRAVELING WITH KIDS

By Dani Rosenblad James

Traveling with kids can be an adventure in itself. Depending on their age, you might need to bring a big bag just for the little one's toys, diapers, food, etc. But there are some great tips that I can give you to help lighten your load!

1. Pre-Plan your Trips!

When traveling with kids it's important to pre-plan trips, especially if you are going to travel internationally. This lessens the stress of keeping the little ones happy since you already have a plan in the works. It's good to know that sometimes a plan can fall through. This doesn't mean all is lost though. Take a deep breath and relax, it will work out. Plus, the kids can pick up on your mood. So, if they see you panicking, they are more than likely going to do the same.

- Research kid-friendly destinations, accommodations and activities
- Keep the itinerary flexible and allow the unexpected or unknown fun moments

2. Pack Smart and Strategically

Thinking before packing your bags and the little ones will have the trip going smoothly. When traveling with kids, snacks are essential. Another thing that's good is an extra pair of clothes, wipes, favorite toy and some entertainment. This could be books, games, or tablets, whichever works best for your family. Something that I feel should be with you at all times when you have kids is a carry-on survival kit. This is great when you are on flights, car rides, and train travel.

3. Engage Kids in the Process

Have your children involved as you are working on planning, or packing for the trip. This could be that the kids are helping you choose the activities or places to visit. Besides that, you can have them help you pack the bags and give them some options so that they feel they helped. While you are working together, explain to them what to expect while traveling, especially if this is the first trip for them.

4. Stick to Routines When Possible

While I have traveled with my son, I have found that staying on a routine is essential. This helps the kids with sleeping well, eating regularly and gives them somewhat of a consistency while traveling. Some kids will feel better when they have a familiar item to help them feel comfortable in new places. This could be a stuffed toy or a favorite blanket.

5. Be Prepared for Downtime

Now, kids can tucker out faster than adults. So plan for breaks during the day for the little ones. Plus, be sure to plan activities that are around nap time and that you have places that can be more relaxing during these times. That could be hanging out at the beach, parks, or museums for the kids.

Travel with the Kids

Above all, remember to have an open mind. It's okay to let loose and be a kid too! That way your little ones and you will have a great time and you'll see the world in a different way! Sometimes it's nice to see the world from a kid's point of view! Be sure to give yourself grace. Not everything can follow a guide note by note. So if things get off plan, it's okay! It's all new experiences and they are things to learn from. You can learn more about traveling with kids at **www.misfitwanders.com**.

A CONVERSATION WITH THE 'QUEEN OF AIR FRYERS,' CATHY YODER

by Merilee Kern, MBA

Widely regarded as the *"Queen of Air Fryers,"* Cathy Yoder—a mother of eight—wanted to prove that air fryers could do more than reheat frozen foods and leftovers. So, she documented her journey on YouTube. Now—with nearly 730,000 subscribers, over 6 million video views and 35,000 cookbooks sold—her channel and thought leadership platform draws over a million monthly visitors, fuels speaking engagements, attracts marquee sponsors, and drives significant affiliate revenue.

As an influencer in the digital marketing world, she has also utilized her experience and knowledge to guide other aspiring bloggers and marketers. She frequently shares valuable insights and strategies that have proven to be instrumental in her own success. With remarkable ingenuity, tenacity, and an uncanny knack for anticipating trends, her viral YouTube videos and influential status within the digital marketing community continue to make her a force to be reckoned with in the world of online content creation.

However, most important to her air fryer empire is that Cathy empowers hundreds of thousands of people to dust off their air fryers and embrace using them to make simple, delicious meals in minutes. With this in mind, and the holiday cooking and gifting season on fast approach, we caught up with Cathy to discuss how she can help make celebratory meals quicker, easier and healthier by using an air fryer as well as the profound success realized through her entrepreneurship, digital marketing and social media influencer endeavors.

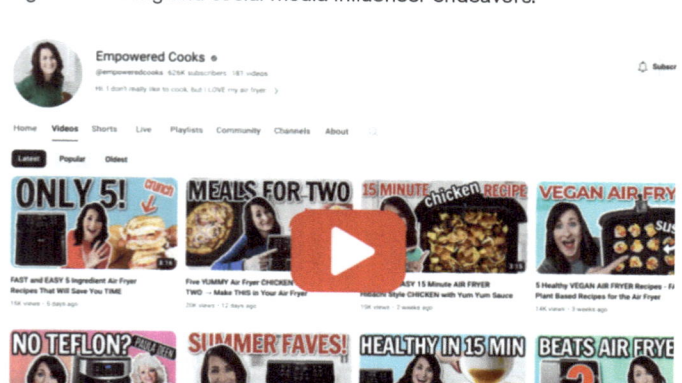

MK: You are a mother of eight, and it's been said that you don't like to cook? Is that what made using the air fryer appealing to you?

CY: Yes, that's true. I don't like to cook. But, as a busy mom of eight kids, I needed a way to put food on the table fast--several times a day. I tried meal prep, delivery services, eating out (not good), and more. Nothing worked. Meal prep required too much time in the kitchen. And the other options were too pricey for my deal-seeking nature. That's when I started experimenting with an air fryer—which also appealed to my penchant for new technology. Soon, I discovered I could make simple, delicious, and mostly nutritious meals in minutes. When my kids ate those first dinners without complaining, I had an *"aha moment"* that dramatically changed how I cook and the trajectory of my business.

In 2020 during the pandemic, with a house full of family members needing to eat, I used my phone to record videos of the food I cooked in the air fryer. The kids tried and rated each recipe. Some even pitched in to help chop, mix, and measure. I posted the videos and recipes on YouTube, and here we are.

I now have a family full of air fryer enthusiasts. The recipe portion of Fabulessly Frugal, which is my original business started to help families save money while enjoying delicious meals, has grown so much that we spun off the cooking content into a site called Empowered Cooks. As a complement to that, I also launched Pine & Pepper, which is a physical product line of cooking accessories. Ironically, my reluctance to cook was an essential ingredient for building this thriving culinary business that helps people (like me) feel more confident in the kitchen.

MK: I understand your Empowered Cooks multimedia platform is designed to guide everyday home cooks on the use of air fryers. What will folks find there?

CY: At Empowered Cooks online, my *"Air Fryer Recipes"* cookbook filled with over 150 recipes is available. To date, it has sold over 35,000 copies worldwide, giving folks the confidence and inspiration to enjoy all that an air fryer has to offer. Other resources on the EmpoweredCooks.com platform include access to an air fryer cooking catalog with over 300 video recipes, accessories, a transformative video course, and interactive cooking class sessions where new and experienced air fryer enthusiasts gather with me to cook and chat as we air fry foods in real time! Overall, this platform motivated home cooks to learn the basics of air frying and feel empowered to experiment with more recipes as they progress with the appliance.

MK: Also a prolific social media influencer, your YouTube channel, itself, boasts over 730,000 subscribers. What resources to you provide there?

CY: On my YouTube channel users will find endless air fryer inspiration! I share easy, delicious ways to make the most of your air fryer. With it, I'm on a mission to empower everyday cooks like me to feel more confident in the kitchen. With simple ingredients and easy-to-follow instructions, every air fryer recipe on this channel will help you make delicious, and mostly nutritious, air fryer meals in minutes. We make recipes ranging from amazing air fryer chicken to salmon, steak, veggies, baked goods, and desserts in a fraction of the time it normally takes. Some of my most popular videos include "4 of THE BEST Air Fryers in 2023--And What to AVOID," 15 Things You DIDN'T KNOW the Air Fryer Could Make, "Top 12 AIR FRYER MISTAKES," and "These 15 Recipes Will MAKE YOU WANT an Air Fryer."

MK: To what do you attribute your book, *"Easy Air Fryer Recipe Book: Best Airfryer Cookbook Recipes for Beginners to Advanced,"* having realized such tremendous success?

CY: Yes, the book project has been such a joy. Inside, readers find more than 150 easy and delicious recipes complete with gorgeous photos. This includes delicious, healthy and effortless meals conveniently organized into six sections: Breakfast, Main Dishes (grouped by protein), Veggies & Sides, Snack & Sandwiches, and Desserts. At the end of the book, you'll find additional quick tips, cheat sheets, conversion charts, and other resources.

Overall, this book is written to transform your air fryer into your all-time favorite kitchen appliance, and teach you how to use your air fryer to create recipes everyone will love. Yummy Air Fryer Recipes isn't full of complicated recipes or crazy ingredients. Each recipe is simple enough for anyone to make, and includes pictures. Plus, the index is arranged to help you quickly find recipes in different categories and ingredients so that you can easily use items you already have on hand in your fridge or your pantry.

If you want to up-level what you make in your air fryer, Yummy Air Fryer Recipes is the cookbook recipe book providing simple-to-follow recipe guidelines getting you top notch results every single time.

AIR FRYER RECIPES

150+ YUMMY AIR FRYER RECIPES

Including Dinner, Sides, Breakfast, Snacks, Lunch & Desserts

BY CATHY YODER

MK: You mentioned that you also offer kitchen accessories and resources—what's available for sale?

CY: Through our Pine & Pepper online eCommerce store that's linked with Empowered Cooks, we offer nearly 30 helpful tools, books and recipe resources —some available for as little as 99 cents—to help users make air frying simple, accessible and to get food on the table fast. One of my favorites is a handy magnetic air fryer cheat sheet, which is designed to help prevent overcooked food, helping users cook over 85 foods to perfection. There are also gadgets like the Mistifi 6-ounce Oil Spray Bottle; Premium Air Fryer Liners Premium Air Fryer Liners and an Instant Read Food Thermometer.

MK: I believe Fabulessly Frugal has an app as well. Tell us about that.

CY: Yes, shopping smart has never been easier. The Fabulessly Frugal app is a mobile database of the best online deals available. Users get deal alerts when you select your favorite brands, shopping categories, or products. And you get access to a price comparison tool that ensures you never fall for *"marketing math tricks"* again.

And, of course, there is the paperback cookbook as well as a wide range of general and specialized digital recipes books—all under $8—available for immediate download. From protein-focused, dessert, kid-friendly, pizza pleasers and meals for two, to diabetic, gluten-free, vegetarian and dairy-free recipe books, we have something for everyone.

For those who really want to dig in, there's also my *"Air Fryers Unleashed! Digital Course"* as well as the *"Cooking with Cathy"* 6-month subscription.

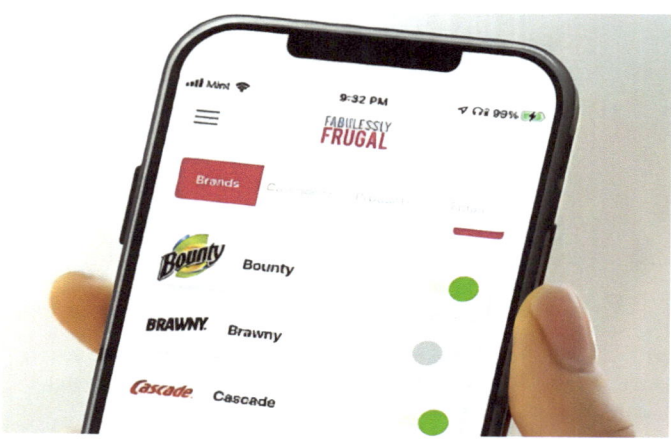

MK: What does the *"Cooking with Cathy"* 6-month subscription entail?

CY: This is a really exciting, immersive option that provides 6-Months of live online cooking classes designed to help participants make fast, delicious, and easy air fryer meals in the comfort of their own kitchen. It's about so much more than just following a recipe; it's about having a group of people to share it with. Our *"Cooking with Cathy Community"* allows users to actively participate, learn, ask questions and get premium support when needed. The format is an online Zoom class with recipe cards to print at home. The subscription provides a monthly live cooking show plus access to past recorded shows.

MK: You had published findings from a survey you conducted unveiling insights into air fryer enthusiasts' preferences—what did you glean from that?

CY: The insights gained from that survey, conducted among our audience of nearly 650,000 subscribers, were compelling, with participants representing a diverse audience demographic. This ranged from empty nesters to a growing cohort of younger enthusiasts between their teens and mid-20s. Among the findings, the survey revealed that owning an air fryer led to faster and more efficient cooking for well over half (67.8%) of users, a shift towards healthier cooking for 44.5%, and increased culinary experimentation for 43%. The usage pattern indicated that 39.7% utilize the air fryer several times a week, 36% use it daily or almost daily, and 9.6% use it once a week. It's been amazing to get these survey results. The insights are opening up new ways for us to support our air fryer community. It's pretty cool to think that air fryers, once just a gadget for zapping frozen foods, have become a kitchen game-changer. We're here to keep bringing everyday cooks the best tips, recipes, and advice, whether they're just starting with an air fryer or have been experimenting with it for a while. It's awesome to be part of the journey with this fantastic kitchen innovation.

In all, Cathy and her multi-faceted Empowered Cooks and Pine & Pepper platforms are bringing the delight of air frying to countless kitchens—and her overarching business insights are inspiring other aspiring entrepreneurs. She's thoughtfully curated a collection of high-quality kitchen tools and recipe books designed to help you prepare air fryer meals quickly and easily, without sacrificing flavor or quality.

In all, Cathy's endeavors are making every day air fryer cooking fun and accessible for everyone, transforming kitchens in a place of joy and creativity.

CONNECT WITH CATHY

www.empoweredcooks.com

EMBRACE CHANGE AND UNLOCK SUCCESS IN 2025

by Paula C Lamb

CONGRATULATIONS—you made it into another year! With the challenges of 2024—economic stress, personal struggles, and global unrest—surviving is no small feat. For many, 2024 was possibly a mix of tough moments and unfulfilled goals. But guess what? the finish line is always moving. Whether 2024 was a win or a struggle, 2025 brings a fresh start, and an opportunity to embrace a new beginning.

Embrace the New Year as Your Moment of Power

The present moment is your point of power. A successful year isn't just about setting goals; it's about embracing change, taking action, and committing to renewal and self-transformation. This New Year instead of chasing fleeting happiness, cultivate a deeper, unshakeable joy that remains constant, no matter life's ups and downs.

As Gary Goodridge said, *"Don't strive to be well-known, strive to be worth knowing."* Success begins with who we are and how we show up in the world. To help you find fulfillment and joy in 2025, I offer a 5-step guide for embracing this new year.

Step 1: Focus on Your Spiritual Journey

This first step may seem unexpected, but focusing on your spiritual self first is essential.

We are made of spirit, soul, mind and body—each part essential to the whole. While we often prioritize our mental or physical health, nurturing your spiritual self is just as important. Connecting with something greater—whether God, the universe, or a higher power—it transforms your mindset, attitude, and actions.

For me, this means prayer, reflection, and connecting with a like-minded community. A strong spiritual foundation brings lasting peace and joy.

Step 2: Embody and Inspire Hope

Hope is essential. It's about believing in renewal and transformation—not just in the world but in your own life.

Take time to reflect on areas where you need hope—relationships, work, or personal growth—and let that hope inspire action toward positive change.

Also, look for ways to inspire hope in others. Even small acts of kindness can ignite hope in someone else's life.

Step 3: Live Out Peace with Others

Peace is not just the quiet within—it's also how we live with others. How can you cultivate peace in your life? Consider what's stealing your peace right now. I encourage you to let go of stress, forgive others, and seek moments of stillness to reconnect with your inner calm.

When you embody peace, you spread it to those around you.

Step 4: Spread Joy Wherever You Go

This New Year be joyful and excited in the anticipation of good things to come—whether it's the opportunity for a fresh start, the end of what was a challenging year. It's the feeling of excitement and positivity about what lies ahead.

How can you practice joy and commit to spreading Joy each day?

Step 5: The Power of Love

The final step is the power of love. Reflect on how you can express love in 2025—not just through grand gestures, but through everyday acts of kindness. Love has the power to heal, connect, and transform lives—both for others and for yourself. I invite you to take one small action each day that reflects love. Whether it's a kind word, a listening ear, or a thoughtful gesture, love is something you can share every day.

Conclusion: Live These Values in 2025

I invite you to live out hope, peace, joy, and love this year. Let these values guide you through 2025, making each day meaningful and connected.

"May you find peace in the stillness, hope in the darkness, love in every moment, and joy in every encounter."

CREATIVITY UNLEASHED: TURNING IDEAS INTO IMPACTFUL ACTIONS

by Courtney Barriger

You have a great idea. A purposeful one that gives you fire and unfolds a thousand paths before you. The problem? Ideas are easy, you sit through scores of ideas from friends and family members every holiday. The problem is that bringing a new idea to life is terrifying.

Where do you start? Who do you bring in for help? How to do you get people to believe your idea when you don't feel you are an expert yet? The biggest obstacle that stops people from pursuing new ideas is imposter syndrome.

This new year, 2025, for me is the birth of a five year incubated idea. And trust me, it is painful. I started writing my book ReFashion Workshop, The Planet Healing Mindset after launching an eco/ethical clothing line Holding Court that required months of research to get right. All of that research went into this book, exploding with possibility, and I brought in scientists, activists, meditation gurus, everyone I could think of to help.

The actions I took to bring about my idea started quietly, while I gained the knowledge I needed to become an expert. Sometimes I would blog about something extraordinary I learned, I started publishing a podcast of the interviews I took as I studied from the best about what sustainability means to the people on top.

As I became an expert, so did the people who followed my social media. It has been a five year journey to test with my audience what they responded to. I find that the most impactful posts are the ones that you are the most passionate about. People can feel it resonating from you. And now as I prepare to launch ReFashion Workshop, my idea of becoming an expert at sustainable fashion is now a reality, and everyone knows it.

Overcome your imposter syndrome by taking it slow. Take small steps on that path, make a plan of action that has a checklist of actions you can take, that has room to grow. Start as a whisper and then turn it into a stage.

Good luck, and keep dreaming!

CONNECT WITH COURTNEY

www.instagram.com/courtneybarriger
www.instagram.com/refashionworkshop
www.refashionworkshop.com
www.holdingcourtinc.com

EMPOWER**HER**
VIRTUAL SUMMIT 2025

When: January 23-25, 2025
Where: Exclusively on FENIX TV
Tickets: $49.97

Be part of the EmpowerHER Virtual Summit 2025, a transformative 3-day event designed to empower women entrepreneurs! Hosted by She Rises Studios, this summit features 50+ expert speakers sharing strategies, stories, and tools to help you break barriers, grow your business, and lead with confidence.

Why Watch?

- Access powerful insights from top women leaders.
- Learn strategies to grow your business and achieve success.
- Be part of a global movement supporting women entrepreneurs.

DON'T MISS OUT—GRAB YOUR TICKET NOW AND IGNITE YOUR SUCCESS!

THINK TRANSFORMATION, NOT RESOLUTIONS

by Glen Alex

Oh boy! It's that time again when so many people make resolutions, usually to go on a diet or to start working out. While resolutions may be filled with good intentions to enhance your life, most are abandoned by the end of January. In fact, research by fitness app Strava found that most people give up on their resolutions by January 19th, which they call *"Quitters Day".* Talk about being short-lived.

Well, if you want more of the same then keep making these empty promises to yourself. If you want a more fulfilling life, then think transformation and not resolutions.

Transformation is a fundamental change or shift, a metamorphosis if you will. Real, effective, and lasting change requires more than 19 days and goes deeper than superficial desires. While losing weight, working out, and saving money are great ways to enhance your life experience, they only scratch the surface. Thus, if you don't go further inside then you are more likely to give up and give in to habitual ways of being.

If you truly desire to slim down, be more active, be healthier, improve finances, or have healthier relationships, then you must transform the beliefs that create and maintain the conditions you're unhappy with. Resolutions just don't cut it; they don't go deep enough.

I had a client who wanted bariatric surgery because her many resolutions to diet and lose weight failed. She was required by the surgeon to get a psychological assessment to address her issues with food before the procedure. Our sessions revealed that her relationship with food was the root of her overeating. My client's belief that food was the only source of love and connection with her family and friends led her to eat large portions, eat when full, and overeat junk food.

Only when my client acknowledged and examined her underlying belief, she able transform it to know that food was not her only source of love. Post-op, she controlled her portions, said "no" to the wrong foods, and stopped eating when full. My client opened up to new ways of experiencing genuine love and kept the weight off. She transformed her beliefs about food and changed her life.

Transformation is an internal realignment of your beliefs and values. Inherent in this realignment is a steadfastness that doesn't require drummed up motivation nor external pressure. Transformation involves genuine commitment that endures setbacks and plateaus. You will flow with the change process rather than resist it. And when you shift your beliefs, your thoughts and behaviors adapt accordingly.

Point your intention toward transformation and away from resolutions. Those false promises are superficial, fleeting, and set you up for failure. Please sit with that for a moment.

Resolutions do not work. If you really want change and improve your life, then you must acknowledge and accept that transformation is the way to better health, more joy, meaningful relationships, and an abundance of goodness. This the first step in the transformation process. And I encourage you to work with a health and wellness professional, like myself, on the next steps. A life or health coach, psychotherapist, or other health expert who addresses your wholeness can guide you to success.

As a Licensed Clinical Social Worker, Author, and Podcast Host, my work is about total health and the whole person. My mission is to help you be joyful, connected, confident, and complete, the life experience I call WELLTH, which is health + other riches.

To achieve wellth in 2025, be like my client and think transformation. Not resolutions.

LET'S CELEBRATE

NEW YEAR, NEW VISION: HARNESSING YOUR UNIQUE POWER TO MAKE 2024 A YEAR OF IMPACT

by Danielle Thompson, Ph.D.

As we step into a new year, the phrase *"New Year, New Vision"* resonates with endless possibilities. But crafting a transformative vision isn't just about setting lofty goals or dreaming big—it's about anchoring that vision in clarity, self-awareness, and intentional action. Over the years, I've seen how the most impactful changes in our lives and communities come from a profound understanding of our unique strengths and how we channel them into meaningful work.

Redefining Success Through Self-Awareness

The world often tells us what success should look like: climbing the corporate ladder, hitting specific milestones, or achieving societal expectations. But true success is deeply personal. It begins with asking ourselves: What impact do I want to have? What unique skills and qualities can I bring to the world? This is the foundation of my work with the Seismic Imprint project, which celebrates individuals who've harnessed their authenticity to make a positive difference.

Each of us has a *"seismic imprint"*—a distinct and powerful way we influence our environments. By aligning our intentions with this intrinsic power, we not only transform our lives but also leave a meaningful legacy.

Setting Transformational Goals

Goal-setting often feels like a chore, weighed down by external pressures or unrealistic expectations. This year, let's reframe that narrative. Goals should be rooted in your values, reflective of your unique vision, and adaptable to the unpredictable currents of life.

Here are three practical steps to set goals that matter:

- **Identify Your *"Why"***: Tie every goal to a deeper purpose. Why does this matter to you? How does it align with your larger vision?
- **Break It Down**: Transform overwhelming dreams into manageable, actionable steps. Progress, no matter how small, builds momentum.
- **Celebrate the Process**: The journey is as important as the destination. Take time to recognize your growth along the way.

Manifesting Change Through Intention

The power of intention is often underestimated. While goals provide structure, intentions breathe life into them. They are the emotional and spiritual fuel behind your actions. In my work, I've seen how embracing intention allows individuals to navigate uncertainty and focus on what truly matters.

A simple practice to start 2024 with intention:

Write down three words that embody how you want to feel this year. Let these words guide your decisions, shaping your vision from the inside out.

Inspiring a Ripple Effect

One of the most beautiful truths about creating a bold vision is that it doesn't stop with you. Your courage to act inspires others to do the same. This is the ethos behind the Seismic Imprint project: when individuals step into their unique power, they catalyze waves of positive change in their communities and beyond.

As women entrepreneurs, leaders, and creatives, we have an extraordinary opportunity to redefine the narrative for 2024. Let this be the year we embrace our individuality, align our visions with our values, and take deliberate steps toward the futures we want to build.

The world needs your vision, your passion, and your action. Whether through entrepreneurship, creativity, or personal growth, 2024 holds the potential to be the year we collectively redefine what's possible. As you craft your goals and intentions, remember that your imprint matters—not just to you but to everyone you touch.

This January, let's step into the new year with clarity, purpose, and the unwavering belief that our vision has the power to transform not only our lives but the world around us.

CONNECT WITH DANIELLE

www.seismicImprint.com
www.instagram.com/seismicimprint
www.facebook.com/profile.php?id=61564060739412
www.tiktok.com/@seismic.imprint
www.linkedin.com/posts/seismic-imprint

YOU CAN'T OUTWORK A BAD MINDSET—HERE'S HOW YOU CAN FIX IT

by Allison Maslan, CEO and Founder of Pinnacle Global Network

Do you want to know what's constantly in the minds of entrepreneurs? It's *"how do I scale?" "I want to hit that goal," "My next milestone should be this and that."* The not-so-good news is none of that happens without the right mindset.

Success doesn't start with perfect strategies or flawless execution—it starts with the way you think. Your mindset is the foundation of every decision you make and every challenge you overcome. The good news is you can shift your mindset anytime to align with the outcomes you want to achieve.

My experience as an entrepreneur and mentor to thousands of CEOs has shown me that those who view challenges as opportunities for growth move forward and scale far faster than those who see them as obstacles and keep retreating to the drawing board.

These mindset shifts will equip you to overcome obstacles and capitalize on the opportunities 2025 has in store for you and your business.

Turn Your Fear Into Focus

Fear is something no one talks about enough in business, yet it's always lurking in big decisions, risks, and unknowns. I think it's important to put out there that fear isn't something you can avoid and that you shouldn't run from it. Fear can be your greatest ally if you know how to work with it.

When I was scaling one of my first businesses, I had monsters within me—fear of making the wrong call, of losing what I'd built, of disappointing my team. However, I learned that fear often points to what matters most. It's like a highlighter for the areas in your business or life that need your attention.

The next time fear shows up, instead of trying to silence it, get curious about it. Ask yourself, What am I really afraid of here? Sometimes, just naming it takes the edge off. Focus on what's within your control. Fear loves uncertainty, but action creates clarity. Turn fear into a signal for where you need to focus your energy, and you'll find it's less of an enemy and more of a guide.

Practice Planning, Not Panic

When things go wrong—and they inevitably will—it's easy to spiral into reaction mode. But reacting from a place of panic rarely leads to good decisions. Instead, you need to slow down and shift into planning mode.

For me, planning is about creating space to respond thoughtfully rather than react impulsively. It's about breaking down big challenges into manageable steps, so they don't feel so overwhelming.

Here's how I keep myself grounded:

- **Pause before you act.** Take a moment to breathe, regroup, and assess the situation before rushing into solutions. Zoom out and look at the bigger picture to get a better view of the situation.
- **Break it down.** When something feels too big to handle, break it into smaller pieces. Focus on the next right step, not the entire solution to the whole problem.
- **Stay connected to your vision.** Remind yourself why you're doing this in the first place. That clarity helps quiet the noise.

Panic is a natural response, but it's not where breakthroughs happen. Planning is what keeps you steady, focused, and ready to move forward with purpose.

Transform Worry Into Action for a Breakthrough Year

Worry has a sneaky way of creeping into every corner of your life, especially when you're building something big. But here's the thing: worry is only useful if it leads to action. Otherwise, it's just wasted energy.

When I feel worry building up, I don't let it sit there and fester. I get it out of my head and onto paper. I write down every concern, no matter how small, and then I look at each one and ask: *What can I do about this right now?*

Some worries will have immediate solutions; some won't. And that's okay. The goal is to take ownership of what you can control and let go of what you can't.

Here's a practice I often recommend:
1. Write down your top three worries.
2. Next to each one, jot down the smallest action you can take to address it.
3. For anything you can't control, make the conscious decision to let it go.

The year ahead is full of possibilities, but the outcomes you achieve will depend on the mindset you choose to bring into it. Fear, panic, and worry don't have to control you. Let 2025 be the year you lean into these shifts.

Get a mentor or someone to call you out when you stray off course. Someone that will call you on your stuff and help to level you up.

The future belongs to those who are willing to think differently, act boldly, and trust their ability to adapt. As you step into this new year, make sure your mindset is focused on creating the success you know you are capable of. When you get your mindset right, everything else will follow. Make 2025 your most impactful year yet!

CONNECT WITH ALLISON

www.pinnacleglobalnetwork.com
www.instagram.com/allisonmaslan
www.facebook.com/allisonsfans
www.x.com/allisonmaslan
www.linkedin.com/in/allisonmaslan

MANIFESTATION MAGIC:
HOW TO SET INTENTIONS AND CREATE THE LIFE YOU WANT IN THE NEW YEAR

by Tracy Worthington

Have you ever felt like you are just living on autopilot? Like each day blends into the next, and no matter how hard you try, you're not quite getting where you want to go? I want to let you know, you are not alone. Many of us start a new year feeling stuck or unsure about how to move forward. But what if I told you that by changing how you think about your life, you can actually change your life?

Welcome to the power of manifestation and intention setting.

What Is Manifestation, Really?

Manifestation is a buzzword these days, but at its core, it's simple: it's about focusing your thoughts and energy on what you want instead of what you don't want. It's not just daydreaming or wishing for things to happen; it's about combining a clear intention with real action.

Think of your brain as a GPS. If you don't program it with a destination, it will just wander aimlessly. But when you set a clear goal and write it down, your brain starts finding ways to make it happen. That's the magic of manifestation—it's not hocus-pocus; it's focus.

The Power of Intention

Let's break it down. An intention is a decision about how you want to live or feel. Unlike a goal, which is something specific you want to achieve, an intention is more about the why and how behind what you're doing. This is probably the most important part of setting an intention.

For example:
* Goal: *"I want to lose 20 pounds."*
* Intention: *"I want to feel strong, healthy, and confident in my body."*

See the difference? Intentions help you tap into your deeper desires. When your goals are rooted in clear intentions, they're easier to stick with.

Why the New Year Is the Perfect Time to Manifest

The start of a new year feels like a blank page in a book. It's a chance to rewrite your story, leaving behind what no longer serves you and stepping into what excites you. That's why so many people make resolutions, but here's the thing: resolutions often fail because they focus on what's *"wrong"* or *"missing."*

Manifestation flips the script. Instead of starting with a list of what you need to fix, you begin by imagining how you want to feel.

How to Manifest and Set Intentions (Step by Step)

Manifesting doesn't require crystals, moon rituals, or anything fancy or woo-woo (unless you enjoy those things, of course!). It's about clarity, belief, and action. Here's how to get started:

1. Get Clear on What You Want

Take a quiet moment to think about what you truly want. Not what you should want, but what lights you up. Write it down. Be specific. Instead of saying, *"I want to be happy,"* try something like, *"I want to wake up every morning excited about my day."*

2. Feel It in Your Bones

Visualization is key. Close your eyes and imagine living that life. What does it feel like? Who's there with you? The more detailed your mental picture, the more you feel the feelings, the stronger the signal you're sending to your brain.

3. Set Daily Intentions

Every morning, take a minute to set an intention for your day. It could be something simple like, *"Today, I will be kind to myself,"* or *"Today, I will focus on progress, not perfection."*

4. Take Aligned Action

Manifestation isn't magic—it's a partnership between you and the universe. Think of it like planting a garden. You set the intention (what you want to grow), but you also have to water the seeds (take action) and pull the weeds (remove doubts and fears).

5. Trust the Process

This is the part most people skip: trust. You may not see results overnight, but keep going. The universe works on its own timeline. Your job is to keep trusting and showing up.

6. Celebrate Small Wins

Every step forward, no matter how small, is proof that your intentions are taking shape. Celebrate those wins—they build momentum.

A Word About Doubt

Let's be honest: we all have had days when we doubt ourselves. It's okay. The trick is to notice the doubt and question it. When we start questioning our fears and doubts, we take away their power. Remember, you don't have to have it all figured out. Manifestation is about progress, not perfection.

What Happens When You Start Manifesting

Once you start setting intentions and aligning your actions, you'll notice little changes. Maybe you'll meet someone who offers exactly the advice you need, or a new opportunity will pop up out of nowhere. That's not luck—it's alignment. When your energy matches your desires, things just click.

Ready to Manifest Your Best Year Yet?

I recommend you start small so you can see proof quickly. This will confirm to your brain that you can do this. Start with setting an intention to find the perfect parking spot or hit all the green lights while driving.

The power to create a life you love is already within you. All it takes is a decision to start. So, grab a journal, find a quiet spot, and ask yourself: What do I really want this year?

Write it down, believe in it, and take the first step. You've got this! Here's to a year filled with intention, action, and endless possibilities.

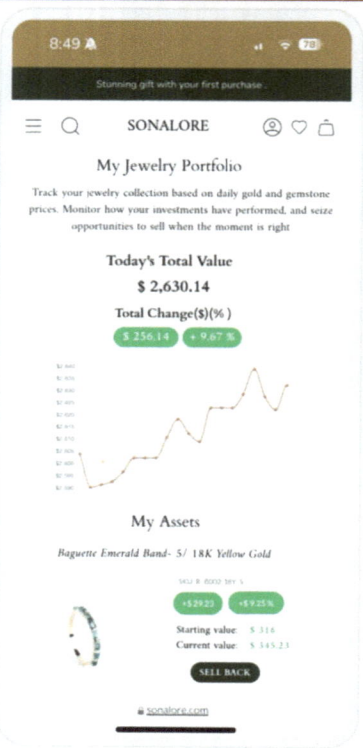

Invest in jewelry you can sell back easily

Monitor your jewelry portfolio and see how it grows in value over time. At anytime, sell it back to us with a click of a button

FROM ACCESSORIES TO ASSETS: PROGRESSIVE E-TAILER REDEFINING VALUE IN GOLD JEWELRY

by Merilee Kern, MBA

Investment, Not Expense: AI-driven eComm platform Sonalore shuns exorbitant retail markups, buys back its gold jewelry at current market value with lifetime guarantee

In today's hugely saturated and competitive jewelry marketplace, distinguishing jewelry retailers can be a challenge for consumers. From lack of brand differentiation, compromised product transparency, value price wars, overlapping product offerings and inconsistent quality assurance to overwhelming digital noise and lack of personal brand connections, many companies in the space struggle to stand out.

One company taking the uber-competitive jewelry retail industry by storm is Sonalore, which has carved out a distinctive identity through a combination of brand discriminators. These include extreme pricing value without the industry standard artificially inflated markups; transparency in their product offerings; exclusive designs crafted by global artisans; ethically and responsibly sourced precious stones and fair wages for its workers; virtual try ons; compelling brand storytelling; and a superior customer experience.

While this mix of USPs is a powerful elixir resonating in the marketplace, perhaps the most noteworthy aspect of Sonalore's approach is that it sells its 18-karat gold jewelry from the perspective of it being a sound investment—not an expense—that enduringly holds its value. This amid the company's robust *"lifetime buyback guarantee"* program based on the fair current price valuation of gold that,

incidentally, has the potential to increase beyond the purchase price of the item. Gold is, in fact, is a heralded investment commodity amid its historically proven performance in various economic environments. Among other drivers, gold investments are known for global demand and liquidity, serving as a tangible asset with no counterparty risk and offering a safe haven during economic turmoil.

Below is a conversation with Sonalore Co-Founders Nidhi Singhvi, who serves as CEO, and Navya Reddy detailing why the brand's approach best serves today's mindful and intentional breed of consumers and investors as well as the modern jewelry retail marketplace at large.

Q: First, how would you describe and explain the Sonalore brand to those unfamiliar?

NS: Sonalore is an AI-powered unified platform for buying and selling fine jewelry, providing upfront, transparent material and crafting cost breakdowns with one click transactability. This is similar to how Carvana revolutionized car sales by offering clear pricing, or how Zillow brought transparency with *"Zestimate"*. Buyers can also confidently purchase jewelry at transparent prices with assurance of a lifetime buyback guarantee. Beyond providing gorgeous jewelry at affordable prices with out ridiculous markups the industry is plagued by, we position gold jewelry as the investment that it is. Customers can sell their items back to the company as easily as they bought it, getting instant and fair buyback valuations higher than comps based on the current market price of gold. Our seamless logistics are also appealing since it helps customers easily refresh their collections anytime.

Q: Your company is built on a model of affordability. What is this founded on?

NR: Yes, the $60 billion unbranded jewelry market is founded on insane markups, often 3 to five times, and are disconnected from the metal content. In fact, most jewelry companies are operating on 65%+ gross margins, so they are not selling gold to you but rather are selling undifferentiated products with absurdly inflated pricing. Our customers also lament that they have jewelry lying around that they don't wear anymore and still have to spend yet more to get new jewelry to enhance and modernize their collections in line with changing personal preferences and trends. We also foster loyalty and trust with our customers by provisioning our pieces with a Certificate of Authenticity akin to other investments. In all, we endeavor to change the fine jewelry market with a unique value proposition of great pricing combined with will utmost product detail transparency—one removing information asymmetry in the jewelry market to foster deep consumer loyalty. This we combine with social responsibility and conscious consumerism via ethically-sourced and made items as well as sustainability via free upgrades and the flexibility to sell back our wares at any time.

Q: What are the main challenges and pain points consumers face when trying to sell their jewelry?

NS: The jewelry re-sell market is value is $30-40 billion, so consumers clearly have this need and desire. But, re-monetizing their jewelry can be a headache via person-to-person attempts or at pawn shops—this noting that our own survey showed fully 90% of people have considered selling their jewelry, but would not feel comfortable walking into a store to do so. Other resale pain points include opaque pricing, where customers receive only 20-60% of the value, and a laborious process involving 2-4 evaluations with a 1-4 week lead time for estimates. Additionally, there is uncertainty around the sale, as many venues are unwilling to hold inventory. The overall anti-luxury experience actively discourages casual sellers from engaging in the process. Our AI powered *"SonaQuote"* buyback tool is quick and transparent. It gives consumers the ability to track the value of their virtual *'jewelry box'* over both time and market movements as well as a one-click sell process whenever the consumer wants.

Q: How have consumer perceptions of gold as an asset evolved in recent years, and how does your product model appeal changing attitudes?

NR: People are increasingly knowledgeable about gold, especially across the U.S., and positioning our products to be "worn then reborn" with a *"buy-enjoy-sell back-repeat model"* is resonating with customers. Jewelry is largely seen as an investment in rest of the world like, in Asia, jewelry is regarded as an asset and bought and sold like one and maintains over 70% resale value as compared to less than 30% in the U.S. Generally, those closely following price action and are aware that gold is currently around $2,700 per ounce. The number one sentiment we hear is, 'gold has been crazy this year, and with all the world's uncertainty, it's only going up.' Many customers also mention how gold prices have significantly increased. While just a few years ago gold was more affordable, now the rising prices make it feel like a more serious investment. Family dynamics also play a big role in gold's appeal, with many regarding it as a cherished heirloom gift from parents with intrinsic fiscal value.

Q: Can you describe your background and how it relates to having established yourself in the jewelry industry?

NS: Navya and I grew up in Asia where jewelry is considered investment. It has been a source of immense self-respect and power for women in a society where women didn't have ownership of other assets and didn't have an income.

Lowest priced fine jewelry you can sell back anytime

BUY. ENJOY. SELL. REPEAT.

VIEW BESTSELLERS

Jewelry was something that was a woman's own treasure chest and, when need be, her own war chest. There are numerous stories in India where women moved their entire families forward using jewelry to fund dreams. Navya have similar stories too—when there was a need to further our experiences, our moms went against other family member wishes and *"made things happen"* realizing the true worth of their jewelry caches. Navya and I want to bring the same power to jewelry in America. Women in the U.S. are spending billions on jewelry, but are not accumulating any intentional wealth with it. We want to turn our customers into gold investors, and help hem pass on this wealth to whomever they want. Sonalore helps women in America do just that and, in doing so, we are truly revolutionizing the jewelry experience. Our products are both a pleasure to wear and smart to own.

Q: OK, let's talk specifically about the gold commodity landscape specifically a bit. Why is gold a smart investment today, even with inflation and cooling prices?

NR: In short, macro uncertainty. The ongoing geopolitical tensions, including two major wars and trade uncertainties, make gold an attractive safe-haven asset, providing stability in investment portfolios during economic challenges. Its historical performance, such as during the 2008 financial crisis, underscores its resilience as a store of value. At Sonalore, 60% of our customers have expressed interest in gold as an investment, reflecting its strong appeal in today's macroeconomic climate. Additionally, major central banks are diversifying away from the US dollar, adding near-record amounts of gold to their reserves in 2023—a trend that signals long-term structural support for gold prices. Gold also offers significant portfolio diversification benefits, particularly for millennials, who now outpace baby boomers and Gen X-ers as the largest group of gold investors. With consistently low or negative correlation to other asset classes, gold remains an ideal tool for reducing portfolio risk.

Q: What economic indicators suggest physical gold will remain a strategic investment in 2025?

NS: Potential rate cuts in 2025 are expected to lower real yields, enhancing gold's attractiveness as an investment since it doesn't bear interest. Additionally, the anticipated *"pivot"* in monetary policy could further drive institutional investors toward gold, viewing it as a reliable hedge against potential currency devaluation.

Q: What do you recommend as the allocation strategy for physical gold?

NR: The optimal strategy depends on the investor's goals. For new investors, it's recommended to focus primarily on coins, allocating roughly 80% of their investment to them. Coins are easier to sell in smaller quantities, providing greater flexibility for partial liquidation, which is ideal for testing the market. For larger investments, a balanced approach with a mix of bars and coins—typically a 60/40 split —is more suitable. Bars serve as long-term core holdings, while coins offer the flexibility needed for quick liquidity.

Q: What would you say are common misconceptions about physical gold investments?

NS: One common misconception about investing in gold is that it is hard to sell. While selling gold may not be as instant as selling stocks, both online and offline platforms offer reliable liquidity options. At Sonalore, we provide unique liquidity for gold jewelry at prevailing gold prices, making it easier for investors to access their investment. Another misconception is that you need a lot of money to start investing in gold. In reality, gold investment can begin with small denominations, such as coins. Additionally, Sonalore allows customers to invest in gold while buying jewelry, such as purchasing 18k gold hoops and watching their value fluctuate with the market.

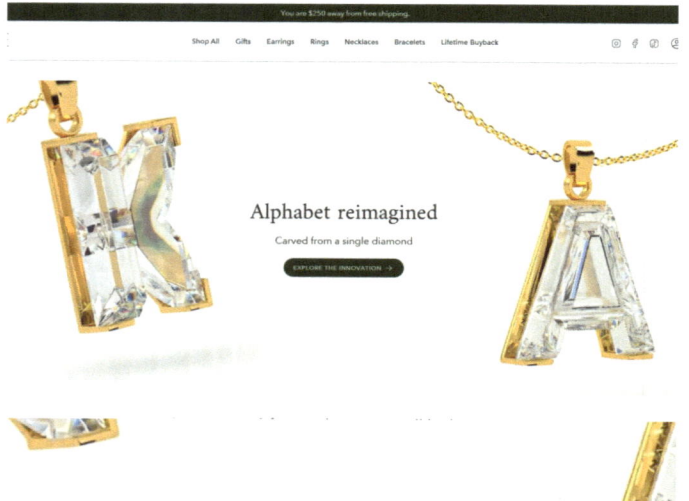

Lowest priced fine jewelry you can sell back anytime

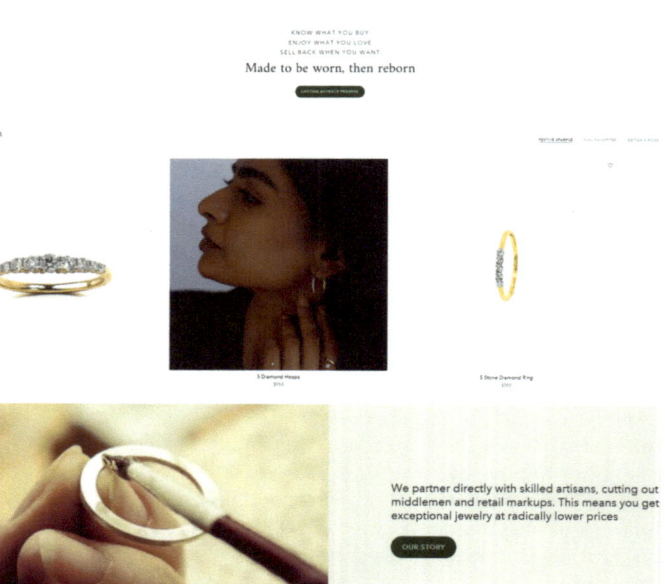

ARE WE ABLE TO BUYBACK JEWELRY?

jewelry has high value of gold and gemstones which we are ha
buyback at anytime

iece? It's recycled into new creations, keeping our cycle sustainable. At Sonalore, your jewelry isn't just beautiful – it's a smar

Q: How would you say investors should think about liquidity in physical gold?

NR: The gold market is highly liquid, fueled by strong institutional and retail demand, with multiple sales channels available both online and offline. Coins offer the quickest liquidity, making them easier to sell to government mints or private buyers. Proper documentation is essential to ensure smooth transactions, and investors should stay informed about market fluctuations to make well-timed decisions. By staying aware of the market, investors can make informed choices that maximize the value of their gold investments.

By positioning gold jewelry as a valuable asset that can be worn and sold back, Sonalore aligns with the growing interest in gold as a hedge against economic uncertainty and as a means of wealth accumulation. Also with a deep understanding of consumer pain points, such as opaque pricing and laborious resale processes, the company's innovative model streamlines the jewelry investment experience, fostering customer trust and loyalty.

In all, Sonalore is redefining the jewelry industry by offering a transparent, customer-centric approach that focuses on both affordability and investment potential. The company's commitment to eliminating inflated markups, providing clear pricing, and offering a lifetime buyback guarantee has resonated deeply with consumers seeking not only beautiful jewelry, but also a smart investment. Hat's off to this innovative startup transforming how consumers view and invest in jewelry, making it both a personal and financial asset for the modern world.

CONNECT WITH NIDHI

www.sonalore.com

A Fresh START FOR January

Written by Hanna Olivas - CEO of She Rises Studios & FENIX TV

A new year dawns, crisp and bright,
With dreams that dance in winter's light.
January whispers, "Begin again,"
A time to rise, to grow, to mend.
In the chill of morning, she finds her way,
With resolve as steady as each new day.
The past year's struggles, she lets them go,
For She Wins by choosing the path to grow.
She knows that kindness is power, true,
That nice girls finish first in all they pursue.
She greets each morning with strength anew,
Ready to face what she must push through.
Others may rush, may scheme, may strive,
But she knows her way to truly thrive.
For the heart that lifts, that shares, that cares,
Finds joy and purpose everywhere.
With open hands and a hopeful heart,
She builds her world, a work of art.
Every act of kindness, a seed to sow,
As she steps into her year, aglow.
January stands, a clean, white page,
Ready to carry her through each stage.
And with each step, her light grows bright,
For She Wins by shining kindness's light.
So here's to fresh starts, to brave, bold dreams,
To kindness sown in winter streams.
Let the year unfold with love in view—
For nice girls finish first, and so will you.

#SheWins #NiceGirlsFinishFirst

www.sherisesstudios.com

EMPTY CANVAS MAGIC PART 2

*The #1 Key Extraordinary Results in 2025 Without Hustle.
A Brain State Altering Fun Process with Pen and Paper*

by Sylvia Becker-Hill

Dear Reader,

Yes, you can dive into Empty Canvas Magic Part 2 without completing Part 1, featured in the December 2024 issue of HANNA. However, if you encounter resistance, procrastination, or self-sabotage while trying this process, it may indicate that Part 1 would help. That installment focuses on releasing stuck emotions from the past year, freeing you to create results effortlessly.

Last month, we explored somatic journaling. This time, we'll play with a unique form of drawing. All you need is a blank sheet of letter-sized paper, your favorite ballpoint pen, and your smartphone to set a timer. The #1 key to producing extraordinary results without hustle is learning how to step into a flow state on demand. This unlocks your creativity and inner guidance with clarity and confidence.

While much flow research focuses on male athletes and peak performance under intense exertion, that's not the flow we're discussing here. Instead, I'm referring to a softer, more feminine flow—a deeply focused state of peace, surrender, and openness where time seems to stand still and the ego dissolves.

To guide you there, I've designed a simple drawing exercise blending intention, somatic movement, and brainwave modulation. Best of all, it only takes 3 to 5 minutes!

Step-by-Step Guide For Your Vision 2025

Step 1:
Write your intention for 2025 in the center of a blank sheet of paper. What do you want clarity on? For example: *"My intention is, to become crystal clear about my focus for 2025, making it a purpose-fulfilling and financially rewarding year."* Use this as inspiration, and don't worry about neatness.

Step 2:
Set a timer for 1 minute. Place your pen on the paper over your intention and let your hand *"dance" freestyle across the page, doodling lines and shapes."* To make this effective:
- Let go of controlling your hand's movements.
- Breathe deeply.
- Keep your intention in mind.
- Follow the pen's tip with your eyes.
- Don't lift the pen until the timer ends.

Step 3:
Reset the timer for another minute. Embellish your drawing—fill in shapes, add patterns, or jot down words and sentences. To make this powerful:
- Don't overthink or analyze.
- Let your eyes follow your hand.
- Add dots, flowers, or spontaneous designs.
- Avoid controlling the outcome; let creativity flow.

Step 4:
Take a few deep breaths. Reflect on your doodle and let answers to your intention flow naturally. Write them in the empty spaces or on the back of the paper.

Step 5:
Take a few more deep breaths and shake out your hands and shoulders. If you feel like it, stand up and shake out your legs and body. Then, sit down, review your drawing, and ask yourself:
- What decision am I making based on these insights?
- What is my first step to implement this decision?

Write down your next step, including a deadline and any supporters who can help.

This process, called Meta-Cognitive Drawing, is part of my Intentional Creativity® toolbox. I use it daily to calm my nerves, activate my brain's hemispheres, unleash creativity, and tap into my inner guidance—whether you call it your muse, intuition, or higher self.
I hope you'll try this method and trust it will bring you wonderful results, just as it has for me and my clients.

Wishing you an extraordinary 2025 filled with peace, ease, and zero hustle.

Warm regards,
Sylvia

AT THE HEART OF A VITAL LIFE

by Debra Hillard

Vitality, the presence of our whole life force, is greater than physical health alone. We tend to live in our minds, operating as if the control center there is in charge of our choices and actions. In truth, the mind is not capable of running the show. It operates on ego, belief systems, programming, like a computer. Without the spiritual component, it tends to run amok. The mind is best used in service to the soul, not in charge of it.

Our mind knows facts, processes input and makes decisions that are often based on all of the ego driven thoughts that tell us who we should be, how we should act, and what our life is supposed to look like, designed to be accepted by others and keep us safe. Our heart tells a different story. It bases its choices on love, passion, and our soul's truth. We are human beings designed with emotions for a reason. When we follow our hearts, knowing our truth and trusting ourselves, we are perfectly guided.

The basis of Shamanism, the spiritual path I follow, is the interconnectivity of all things. Natural forces, the elements of our earth, and the heavens, are thought of as family. Everything has a soul, permeated with essence and consciousness and deserves our reverence. Our work is to find our own soul essence and in doing so, our true power.

Being fully vital and alive, requires the presence of your soul essence, your real power. We need to remember who we truly are and oftentimes, some guidance along the way, is helpful. When we are not living our truth, even success on a worldly stage can leave us feeling empty. The quest for truth can lead to a life of fulfillment and meaning beyond imagination. A life without it, pales in comparison, though on the surface it might appear all glittery and gold.

The work I do was born out of my desire to experience bliss and abundance, not just for a moment, but as a way of life. After years of hardship, illness and loss, I knew I was ready to receive more.

Surrounding myself with things that delight my senses reminds me of the abundance I can receive when I am willing to open the door. And the same is true for all of us. Mother Earth is not lacking in treasure. We must be open to receiving it, to seeing the magic around us and to allowing ourselves to experience it all through our senses. That is the beauty of being human. We feel.

Physical sensation provides access to a deeper experience of yourself and to a path that transcends the mind and transports you beyond the present.

The feeling of bliss when we are touched in just the right way, expands our energy, connecting us to our natural state of love, compassion and joy. In essence, we can feel the opening of our hearts. Some call this rapture.

I have created my own *"Wraptures"* as a way to transport you through their luxurious colors, forms and textures. Each element contains the energy of Spirit transformed into art. The *"canvas"* for each creation has been created with specific attention to the way it drapes over your body, the sensual feel of the fabric, and the emotional response it elicits. You will wrap yourself in their magic and feel your senses ignited. *"Wraptures"* were inspired by Spirit and created by my own heart's desire to share their unique potential.

I invite you to embark on a journey unlike any other.

CONNECT WITH DEBRA

www.facebook.com/dkhillardart
www.instagram.com/dkhillard
www.youtube.com/@dkhillard
www.dkhillard.com
www.dkhillardart.com

THE PERFECT NEW YEARS GIFT!

PUBLISHED BY SHE RISES STUDIOS

Books make timeless gifts, offering stories, inspiration, and a touch of magic. From heartwarming novels to motivational reads and beautifully illustrated coffee table books, there's something for everyone. Give the gift of imagination and joy this Christmas!

THE PERFECT NEW YEARS GIFT!

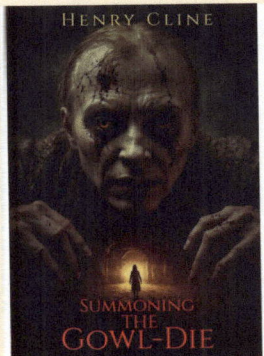

SUMMONING THE GOWL-DIE

Henry Cline

SMALL STEPS, BIG WINS

Susan Saller

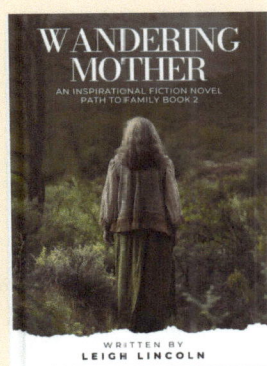

WANDERING MOTHER

Leigh Lincoln

BRIDGING THE DIGITAL DIVIDE

SURVIVING GRIEF & COME BACK TO LIFE

THE PERFECT NEW YEARS GIFT!

SUMMER SOLSTICE

Henry Cline

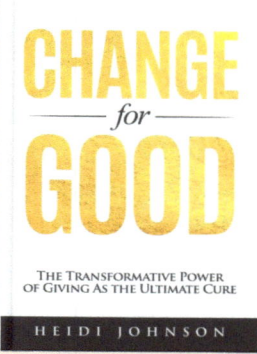

CHANGE FOR GOOD: THE TRANSFORMATIVE POWER OF GIVING AS THE ULITMATE TOOL
Susan Saller

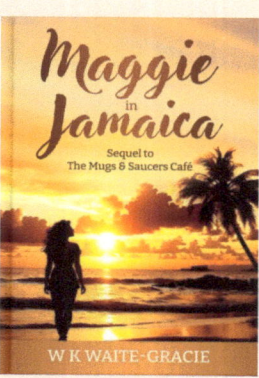

MAGGIE IN JAMAICA

Katherine-Waite Gracie

IS MANIFESTING BULLSHIT: PART 2

SWEET RIDGE HEART
Susan Bagby
(SP Author)

NAUTI GIRL
Stephanie Pavletich-Kraemer

THE PERFECT NEW YEARS GIFT!

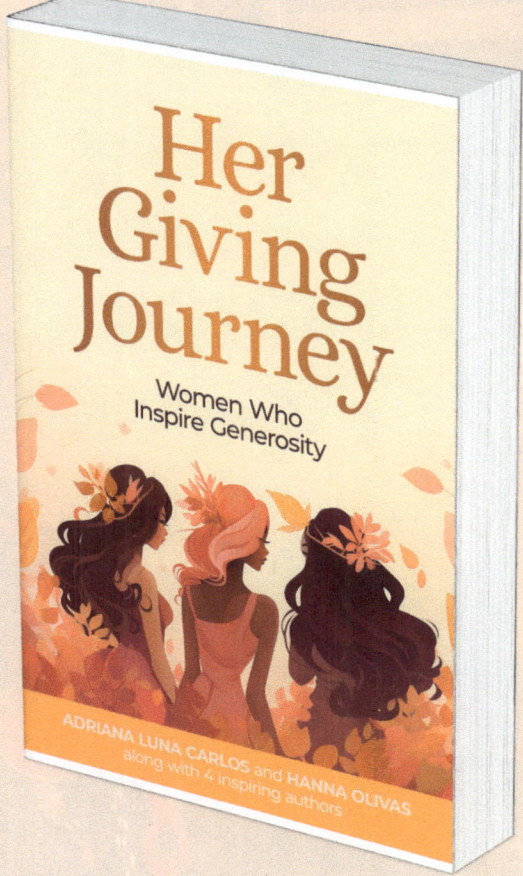

Her Giving Journey: Women Who Inspire Generosity celebrates extraorcinary women whose acts of kindness have sparked meaningful change in their communities and beyond. This inspiring collection features local heroes and global changemakers who used creativity, courage, and compassion to overcome challenges and uplift others.

Through their powerful stories, you'll discover the boundless potential of generosity and reflect on your own capacity for kindness. Join **Adriana Luna Carlos, Hanna Olivas, and four inspiring co-authors—Jennifer Jonassaint, Dr. Sonya A. McKinzie, Krista Sobieski, and Karen Rudolf**—as they motivate you to embrace the spirit of giving and create a brighter, more compassionate future

SHOP NOW ON AMAZON

SHE RISES
STUDIOS

THE POWER OF PUBLISHING
WHY PUBLISH A BOOK, YOU ASK?

Publishing a book is one of the most fulfilling ways to share your story with the world and leave a lasting legacy. It boosts your credibility and highlights your expertise in your industry. Plus, you'll be stepping into the massive $138.5 billion book market industry —and it's still growing!

Best of all, it's easier now than ever before to get your book out there. How exciting is that?

At She Rises Studios, we are on a mission to become the top publishing house for women in the USA. We believe in the power of storytelling to create influencers and stronger communities. We're here to help you break barriers, grow, and make waves in the publishing world.

Get published with us TODAY!

Visit www.SheRisesStudios.com or email us at contact@sherisesstudios.com

I'M JEN RIGLEY, FOUNDER OF FLOURISHING OVER FIFTY

It's January! The hustle and bustle of the holidays is over and we are settling back into our routines. In many areas of the country it is cold and wet, and everywhere the sun is low on the horizon - it's dark when we wake up and when we leave the office. It's also the time when many of us hibernate and are alone with our thoughts. We can start to feel down as we spend less time with others, less time in the sun and less time being active.

But the opposite is also true -- we have more time to dive deep into our desires and focus on activities that are most meaningful to us. A little more me time and a little less time spent on everyone else. A journal, a fire, a bath, a lit candle - how scrumptious is that? I invite you to step into what feels most good to you during these winter days - take the time to pamper, to heal, to cultivate joy in your special way.

There was a time in my life when I was caught up in my own personal vortex - a swirling mass of challenges and change. I was downsized out of my executive position, my mother fell ill, and I faced a breast cancer diagnosis. But as I navigated these hardships, I realized something powerful: even after significant trauma, we can choose to flourish.

That's when the idea of Flourishing Over Fifty, and The Flourish JourneyTM was forged - a vision for inspiration and resources, where women in midlife can come together, lift each other up, hold space and share our stories. When I was facing my hardest moments, I longed for a community like this, a place that felt like home even online.

The Flourish JourneyTM, my framework for overcoming challenges and trauma so you can create a new story for your life has 7 steps, but the first is the most important one - and it fits so well with our winter lives.

Understanding that starting on the path to create a new story for your life is not as easy as *"just change your mindset"*, this process takes you on a journey as you walk through the steps of designing your new story.

This first step in The Flourish Journey ™ is all about creating the foundation. I recommend committing to spending 3 minutes on the following activities to set the foundation for your day:

- **Sit in Stillness** - spend 1 minute quieting your mind and taking some deep breaths. This is when you put your phone in silent mode and turn off the TV.
- **Set your Intention** - spend 1 minute setting your intention for the day. This is not about accomplishing your to-do list, it is more about how you want to feel, or how you want to make others feel.
- **Hold Gratitude** - spend 1 minute thinking, feeling, writing, drawing or painting what you are grateful for.

By committing to these 3 activities each day (just 3 minutes a day), you have the opportunity to change the trajectory not only of your day, but you have the opportunity to change the trajectory of your life.

Flourishing Over FiftyTM is more than an idea, it's a reminder that in midlife, we're just beginning to tap into our true strength. We're here to support, inspire, and help each other through. Here's to our resilience, our joy, and to flourishing over fifty.

Sign-up at *www.flourishingoverfifty.com* to receive our newsletter so you, too, can start creating a new story for your life.

CONNECT WITH JEN

www.instagram.com/flourishingoverfifty
www.facebook.com/flourishingoverfifty
www.flourishingoverfifty.com/subscribe-page

Virtually Angelic Foundation
FOUNDER ANGELA THOMPSON

Virtually Angelic

Who is Angela Thompson you may ask well she's a native from St. Louis. Missouri. A natural leader ready to step up and be a inspiration for everyone. Her hardships made her into the person she is today. Her battles with abuse, cancer, and trauma is what she used to turn her pain into passion for art, children, and wanting to help others. Take a look at this amazing story of the young inspiring entrepreneur.

Virtually Angelic Foundation was a vision that children can have emotional support. Most children are misunderstood when they can't express their feelings so I created a space where children can just be themselves.It's an environment where children can be expressive in a healthy way. Our mission is to provide children with a safe place of belonging to be expressive and give them a better pathway to the future. By using age appropriate activities in the community they can build self esteem, better mental health, and self acceptance. Each month we do events around the community. So children and their friends can build better bonds and getting out in the community to connect with others and have fun!

VirtuallyAngelic Foundation donates each month to the birthday buddies at Cornerstone preschool. We are dedicated to making children feel special on every occasion!

Our foundation is unique because it is self driven we listen to the needs of the children and let them have a voice.

Some of the children participating in the Juneteenth Parade!

We accept donations for children's events through out the year! Including Monetary, clothing,shoes, toys and more!

Contact us!

Phone number 314-967-9023

Email VirtuallyAngelic@outlook.com

website

www.virtuallyangelic.com

RESILIENCE THROUGH FAITH:
TRACI GALLES' JOURNEY OF OVERCOMING ADVERSITY

I'm Traci Galles. I grew up in Grand Rapids Minnesota. I loved my life with my two sisters and brother. I grew up in a very loving household. My dad was a pastor of 4 church's in the state of Minnesota. When I was about 8 yrs old I was molested by a friends nephew. He was a wrestler and told me if I told anyone, he would hurt me physically. Every once in a while, I still get nightmares from that experience. I was a senior in high school when my parents looked at the map and they put their finger on Brainerd, Minnesota. We moved to there in 1994. When I turned 21, I had the mindset to be a virgin until marriage, but that didn't happen because I was raped during that year. At this point in my life, I didn't want anything to do with God. I chose to drink heavily every weekend. I lived with my mom in a small apartment in 1998. She ended up kicking me out because I was up until 4 am and she had to work the next day. I was in contact with a friend that moved to Richmond, Virginia. She wanted me to move out there with her and her boyfriend. I did move there and lived there for seven years. I experienced four natural disasters while I was there. After the fact, I realized that God had me experience those natural disasters because He wanted me to be home in Minnesota where are my family lived. I moved back home September 2008. I worked a couple of jobs in Minnesota but was not very happy. In May 2010 excepted a job offer at Essentia Health, a large hospital in Brainerd Minnesota. I worked there for 10 years and then got laid off because of Covid. I was fine with it at first but then a couple weeks went by and I was devastated. It was one of the hardest, most difficult experience that I've ever dealt with. The loss of my job after 10 years. I spiraled into a deep depression and then a manic episode (highs/lows/some hallucinations). I ended up in the hospital for seven days. It was very difficult for me to be away from my husband (of 10 years) and my daughter. I was really depressed because I had gained 20 pounds because of a medication that I was taking. I was hyper focused on myself instead of others. When you focus on others and their problems and have empathy for them that can help you in your own life. In May 2024 I experienced a severe headache, pain level 10. I was admitted to the hospital for 3 days until they diagnosed me with Lyme disease and meningitis. I left the hospital on the 4th day with pain medication, probiotics and an antibiotic. That following week the ER Doctor called me on my cell number and told me that I needed to go Fargo or Duluth hospital to treat a possible aneurysm. My husband and I decided to have the brain angiogram done at the St Cloud hospital. It came back *"no findings"*. We were really happy about that. I lead a mental health group with my husband that started in 2022. So basically to summarize my story I will say that I have experienced a lot in life. I would like people to know that I am not defined by my circumstances or my diagnosis. I am defined by God, I am a Child of God. Thank you for taking the time to read my story.

CONNECT WITH TRACI
@tracigalles
www.flinckt@yahoo.com

COMING SOON

EV

EMPOWERED
VENTURES

One vision,
countless businesses,
endless empowerment.
Find her here.

womenowned-business.com

Get on the Pre-Launch list!

FAITHFUL FOUNDATIONS: TRANSFORMING NONPROFIT & CHURCH MARKETING WITH MARILYN JEANNE DESIGNS

by Gina Stockdall

In today's world, marketing is more than just a strategy; it's a tool that can amplify the mission and vision of organizations doing Kingdom work. Marilyn Jeanne Designs, founded by Gina Stockdall, offers a unique approach to marketing—one that is rooted in faith and purpose. Their mission is to support nonprofit and church leaders with tailored marketing strategies that align with Christian values. Now, Marilyn Jeanne Designs is taking that mission one step further with the launch of their Nonprofit & Church Faithful Marketing Course.

A Mission Built on Faith

Marilyn Jeanne Designs understands that nonprofit and church leaders have a deep desire to serve their communities and share the Gospel, but often struggle with the complexities of marketing. That's where the course comes in. By combining proven marketing techniques with a strong foundation in Biblical principles, the course is designed to equip faith-based organizations with the tools they need to grow, reach new audiences, and further their impact. The course offers actionable insights on social media marketing, content creation, and much more —all grounded in faith.

The heart of Marilyn Jeanne Designs is to empower Christian organizations to spread their messages of hope, love, and faith effectively. Gina Stockdall, the CEO and Founder of Marilyn Jeanne Designs, has experienced firsthand the challenges that nonprofit leaders face in building a strong, consistent online presence. Her own journey, fueled by the desire to help others thrive in both ministry and business, led her to create this course as a way to empower churches and nonprofits to elevate their outreach efforts and expand their Kingdom impact.

The Nonprofit & Church Faithful Marketing Course

This comprehensive 8-week course is specifically designed to help nonprofits and churches learn how to market their missions effectively while remaining true to their Christian values. The curriculum covers essential topics such as creating a clear message, building an authentic brand, and leveraging social media platforms to engage a community. Each module is carefully crafted with a Christ-centered focus, reminding participants that marketing is not just about sales— it's about serving God's people and fulfilling His purposes.

As the course progresses, students will learn how to connect with their target audience in a meaningful way and develop strategies that will help their organizations grow. They will also have the opportunity to apply what they've learned through hands-on exercises and assignments that reinforce Biblical leadership principles.

Why You Should Register Today

The Nonprofit & Church Faithful Marketing Course is an invaluable resource for church and nonprofit leaders who want to reach more people and build stronger relationships with their communities. As the Bible says in Proverbs 16:3, *"Commit your work to the Lord, and your plans will be established."* This course is a chance to invest in the future of your organization, while aligning your marketing efforts with God's purpose for your ministry.

Enrollment is now open, and the course is available for just $49. Don't miss out on this opportunity to strengthen your marketing efforts and make a lasting impact for the Kingdom.

Register Today

To learn more about the Nonprofit & Church Faithful Marketing Course and to register, visit marilynjeannedesigns.com. Whether you're looking to build a new marketing strategy or refine your existing efforts, this course will equip you with the tools, knowledge, and Biblical guidance needed to succeed.

As Marilyn Jeanne Designs continues to support organizations in their mission to spread God's love, we encourage you to take the next step in strengthening your marketing efforts. Remember, as Philippians 4:13 says, *"I can do all things through him who strengthens me."* With faith and the right tools, anything is possible.

CONNECT WITH GINA

www.marilynjeannedesigns.com
www.facebook.com/marilynjeannedesigns
www.instagram.com/marilynjeannedesigns
www.tiktok.com/@marilynjeannedesigns

THE PATH TO MY FAMILY

by Leigh Lincoln

Since I published the first novel in my Path to Family series, Lost Father, in 2023, the questions *'Why a series on adoption?'* and *'Why a novel about a birth father?'* have popped up. Which, for me, are rather personal questions. And when I'm faced with how best to answer, the only way is to share my story.

See this grainy, old photo here? That's my parents and me, way back when. On my *'gotcha day'* – the day we became a family. The day they got to meet me, hold me for the first time, and know that I'd be one of their kids. Yup, I'm adopted. Not something I usually share, but it's always been a huge part of my life. Adoption has shaped me, changed me, made me who I am.

However, there's another side to the story, the untold story of my origin. Which left me wondering about those missing pieces. Nothing against those two wonderful people who adopted me and raised me as their own. My parents are my parents, I love them with my whole heart. Yet, something in me longed to walk into a room someday and look into the eyes of someone who shared my DNA.

But there wasn't any easy way to figure out the puzzle of my birth, few records, few clues. I pulled on every string I found and spent a whole lot of years of searching. Hit so many disappointing roadblocks. A lot of heartache because I didn't think I'd ever find answers to my questions. Do I have my father's eyes? My mother's nose? And so many more.

Don't worry, this story has a happy ending. I'm one of the fortunate adoptees who found a birth parent and was able to build a relationship. Not all of us adoptees have that type of outcome, either because the reunion doesn't go well or no birth parents are ever found.

My birth father and I are getting to know each other, learn about all of those years between my birth and now. It's been nerve-wracking, wonderful, unexplainable.

Over the years, I've tread lightly around my adoption story and journey. So many didn't understand my viewpoint or made comments that ranged from naïve to borderline cruel. But now that I've become a best-selling author, I've discovered the power my words have to change a few hearts and minds. I'm the best possible person to share the whole picture of adoption – birth father, birth mother, adoptive parents, child.

Thus, when I set out to write a novel about adoption, it grew and became a series. As I researched for the novels by speaking to so many wonderful people, I learned something important. My story isn't unique, unusual, or abnormal. Other adoptees have similar feelings to mine, the longing to connect with a birth parent, the wondering about the reasons behind being given up.

So why this series, why the different viewpoints? Well, put yourself in the shoes of a parent who gave the gift of their child to strangers. And then spend their whole life wondering what happened next. This is the main plot of Lost Father and Wandering Mother. I'm not trying to paint adoption as some perfect Rockwell painting. Because, in the end, sometimes adoption isn't perfect because nothing ever is. There's raw emotion, there's gut-wrenching heartache, there's a loss that can't quite be overcome. And a touch of hope.

And maybe a few people will read the Path to Family series, and discover, pitfalls and all, something good can come out of the most difficult circumstances.

THRIVING IN THE NEW YEAR:
BUILDING RESILIENCE AND ADAPTABILITY FOR SUCCESS

by Carrie Speed

Starting a new year often feels like stepping into a world of endless potential. You craft a vision, set your goals, and feel ready to tackle anything that comes your way. But let's face it—life rarely unfolds according to plan. Challenges come up, circumstances shift, and we're often forced to adapt on the fly.

That's where resilience and adaptability come in. These traits aren't just tools for bouncing back—they're the keys to thriving amid uncertainty. Whether you're launching a new business, pursuing a personal goal, or simply striving for a more intentional life, these qualities will help you stay on course even when the road gets bumpy.

Here are some practical strategies to help build resilience and adaptability as you chase your vision this year.

1. Start with a Strong "Why"
Every vision needs a foundation, and that foundation is your purpose. Why is this goal meaningful to you? How will achieving it enrich your life or the lives of others? When challenges happen (and they will), reconnecting with your *"why"* provides clarity and motivation. Write it down where you can see it every day—a sticky note on your desk, a note in your phone, or a line in your planner. Your purpose is your north star, guiding you when the path isn't clear or when it feels hard.

2. Embrace a Growth Mindset
A growth mindset is the belief that skills and abilities can improve with effort. When obstacles appear, instead of thinking, I can't do this, reframe your perspective. Ask, What can I learn from this? or How can I approach this differently? Viewing setbacks as opportunities for growth builds resilience. It turns failure into feedback, helping you move forward with new insights and strategies.

3. Practice Mindful Adaptability
Adaptability doesn't mean abandoning your goals—it means adjusting your methods. Mindfulness can help you navigate these shifts with intention. When things don't go as planned, pause and take a deep breath. Ask yourself:
- What is within my control right now?
- What adjustments can I make to stay aligned with my vision?

By staying present and open-minded, you can approach change not as a disruption, but as an opportunity for innovation.

4. Build a Resilience Toolkit
Resilience is like a muscle—you can strengthen it with regular practice. Here are a few tools to add to your resilience toolkit:
- **Self-compassion**: Be kind to yourself when things get tough. Instead of self-criticism, practice self-encouragement.
- **Stress management techniques**: Simple practices like deep breathing, meditation, or a quick walk can help regulate your emotions and keep you grounded.
- **Journaling**: Writing about challenges can help you process emotions, gain clarity, and find solutions.

The more you practice these skills, the more naturally they'll come when you need them.

5. Create a Flexible Plan
Rigid plans often crumble under pressure. Instead, think of your plan as a living document—something you can adjust as circumstances change. Set clear goals but allow room for flexibility. For example, if your goal is to grow your business, outline several strategies you can use, such as networking, social media, or partnerships. If one approach doesn't work, you'll have others to fall back on.

6. Lean on Your Support System
Even the most resilient people need support. Surround yourself with a network of friends, mentors, or colleagues who understand your vision and can offer encouragement, advice, or perspective. Sometimes, just talking through a challenge with someone you trust can help you see solutions you hadn't considered. Don't hesitate to ask for help—it's a strength, not a weakness.

7. Celebrate Progress Along the Way
It's easy to focus on the end goal, but resilience comes from recognizing the journey. Celebrate every milestone, no matter how small. Progress is progress, and acknowledging it keeps you motivated. Whether it's finishing a difficult project, hitting a minor benchmark, or simply making it through a tough week, take time to reflect on how far you've come.

Building resilience and adaptability isn't about avoiding challenges—it's about meeting them with confidence and creativity. As you pursue your vision this year, remember that it's okay to stumble, pivot, and start again. The key is to keep moving forward, no matter what obstacles arise.

This year, let resilience and adaptability guide you. With these tools, you'll not only overcome challenges but grow stronger because of them. Let's make this the year we turn our boldest visions into reality.

With joy,
Carrie Speed
Founder, Joyful Rising
Certified Mindfulness & Happiness Coach | RYT-200

CONNECT WITH CARRIE

www.joyfulrising.net

JOIN OUR COMMUNITY

We believe the future is female and that we are better and stronger together. This group is NOT just for entrepreneurs but for women in general of all ages and from all walks of life.

www.bit.ly/srscommunitygroup

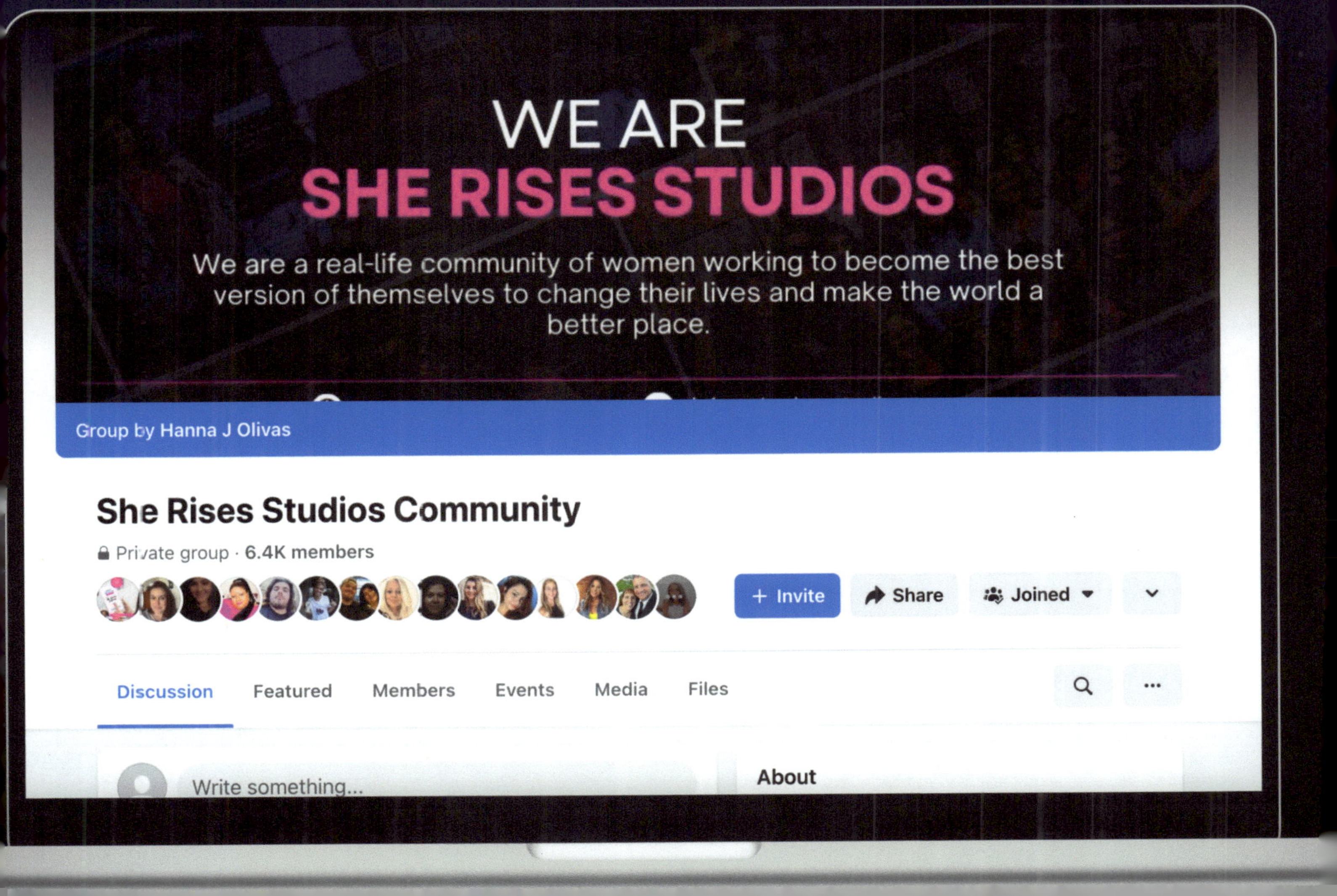

WE ARE
SHE RISES STUDIOS

We are a real-life community of women working to become the best version of themselves to change their lives and make the world a better place.

Group by Hanna J Olivas

She Rises Studios Community

🔒 Private group · 6.4K members

   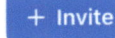 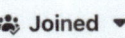

+ Invite　　**↗ Share**　　**👥 Joined ▾**　　**▾**

Discussion　　Featured　　Members　　Events　　Media　　Files　　🔍　　...

Write something...　　　　　　　　**About**

NEW BOOK DARES LEADERS TO RELATE & LEAD WITH A FIERCE HEART

by Merilee Kern, MBA

In the much-anticipated new book, "*Dare to Relate: Leading with a Fierce Heart*," trailblazing former federal agency CEO, TEDx speaker and renowned relational leadership expert Cheryl L. Mason, J.D. unveils an unconventional yet highly effective approach to leadership, In it, she challenges the status quo, encouraging leaders to take *personal responsibility* for their team's engagement and development.

Having been the fourth Presidentially-appointed, Senate-confirmed—and first woman—to serve as the CEO/Chairman of the VA Board of Veterans' Appeals before founding her Catalyst Leadership Management consultancy for which she serves as CEO, in "*Dare to Relate*," Mason provides a refreshing perspective to revolutionize workplace culture and leadership practices to foster a more dynamic, cohesive, productive and effective team environment.

Mason is a visionary who has transformed workplace culture and achieved unprecedented results. Thus, unlike conventional leadership training, "*Dare to Relate*" is written to forge a new path for cultivating strong workforce relationships. It addresses the fundamental principle that employees are people and a company's most valuable resource.

Contemporary leaders often lack the preparedness and essential tools needed to effectively lead today's workforce. All too often, leaders rely on human resources or personnel management to manage their employees. "*Dare to Relate*" challenges the status quo, empowering CEOs and other leaders—both established and aspiring—to take personal responsibility for engaging and investing in the people who comprise their workforce. With this book Mason provides a compass for visionary leaders who dare to create an impact.

"Being a catalyst leader involves facing challenges, overcoming obstacles and genuinely caring for and supporting your employees," says Mason. *"In 'Dare to Relate,' I share my journey and guide readers through essential principles of the relational management style. The book outlines the kind of skills needed to lead with authenticity and empathy. The kind that bolster staff morale, trust and bottom line results in kind."*

From her own journey as a military spouse to her groundbreaking role as the first woman CEO of a federal agency, Mason extraordinary journey detailed in the book is inspirational and empowering. So too are her actionable insights intended to embolden readers to break free from limitations and forge their own path of self-development to realize unparalleled success.

A Peek Inside:

Geese in V Formation:
Mason draws an insightful parallel between the flight patterns of geese and leadership. Have you ever watched geese fly in their distinctive V formation? Mason encourages us to pay close attention, for there's a lesson in true leadership to be learned.

Leadership in Action:
In their flight formation, the leader occasionally drops back to let another take the lead. This selfless act optimizes flying time, showcasing the importance of shared leadership responsibilities.

Efficiency and Communication:
The geese position themselves just above the bird in front, reducing wind resistance and conserving energy. This fosters efficient communication and allows them to track each other, highlighting the power of teamwork.

Purpose, Impact, and Value:
Mason underlines that each member of the flock serves a purpose, impacts others, and brings value to the team. This analogy beautifully illustrates the interconnectedness of leadership and teamwork, emphasizing the importance of caring for the team.

If you or someone you know is keen on a dynamic, inspirational and high-impact book that can ignite the spark of leadership within, look no further than "*Dare to Relate*" as a powerful source of motivation and key learning for building powerful, meaningful and authentic workplace connections.

Available Now!

amazon

BARNES & NOBLE

ELMSTREETBOOKS

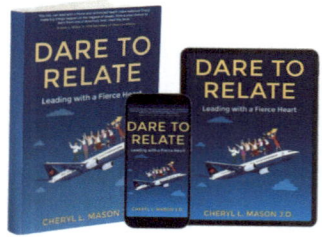

CONNECT WITH CHERYL

www.catalystleadershipmgmt.com

ROBIN DIMOND, CEO & FOUNDER OF FIFTH & COR

Entrepreneurship is often a journey full of uncertainty, challenges, and unexpected turns, yet it's also a path that allows us to push the boundaries of creativity, innovation, and personal growth. As entrepreneurs and leaders, our ability to cultivate resilience and adaptability shapes not only the success of our ventures but also our own personal transformation.

Entrepreneurship is about more than just launching a business; it's about creating a vision that evolves and grows with you. As the founder and CEO of Fifth & Cor, I've learned that the foundation of any successful venture is a vision grounded in purpose. However, what's equally important is the ability to pivot and refine that vision as the market shifts and as we discover new opportunities. In my career, the act of redefining my vision has been a constant practice. Over time, I realized that my passion lay not just in the technical aspects of marketing but in the emotional connections that brands can form with their audiences. It was then that I redefined the mission of Fifth & Cor —blending the latest technologies with immersive, multi-sensory experiences to create marketing that touches both the heart and mind.

As a leader, this adaptability has been crucial. As I navigated through industry shifts and faced new challenges, I knew that to continue growing, I had to remain open to change. True leadership is about evolving with your vision and fostering a culture of innovation within your company—one that encourages others to take bold steps forward.

Creativity is not just about thinking outside the box; it's about challenging the box itself. At Fifth & Cor, our work thrives on innovation, and I've found that the most rewarding projects often start with a bold idea that defies conventional thinking. Innovation is born when we look at a problem from a different perspective. In our work, we harness the power of multi-sensory experiences to create campaigns that engage customers on a deeper level. For instance, we combine immersive digital tools, sensory-triggering elements, and storytelling to craft campaigns that connect with people not just intellectually, but emotionally. It's these bold ideas, these leaps of faith, that often lead to the most powerful transformations.

I've also seen firsthand how courage to innovate builds resilience. The marketing landscape is constantly evolving, and staying ahead of trends requires taking calculated risks. Whether introducing new technologies like spatial computing and AI or experimenting with unconventional marketing tactics, every bold decision has contributed to our success.

On the other hand, personal development is an essential part of leadership and entrepreneurship. It's about aligning your personal growth with your professional ambitions, and understanding that the two are deeply interconnected. One strategy I use is to set goals that aren't just measurable but are aligned with my long-term vision. For example, in the early years of Fifth & Cor, I focused on building relationships and gaining industry recognition. Those milestones were a stepping stone to something much larger—an opportunity to build a team that shares my vision and empowers them to grow alongside the business. Another key strategy is mindfulness. Taking time to reflect, assess, and re-align is critical to staying on track. I make sure to regularly check in with my personal and professional goals to ensure they still reflect what I truly want.

A new perspective is often what separates those who achieve their vision from those who give up when faced with challenges. Developing a resilient mindset is an essential tool in overcoming obstacles and staying focused on the path ahead. One of the most powerful mindset tools I've used is reframing challenges. Instead of seeing a setback as failure, I see it as an opportunity to learn and grow. For instance, when faced with an unexpected setback in a project, I don't ask *"Why did this happen?"* but instead *"What can I learn from this?"* This mindset shift has been invaluable in maintaining resilience.

Throughout my career, I've witnessed countless examples of visionary individuals who turned their dreams into reality through resilience and adaptability. From small business owners to global leaders, the common thread among these individuals is their unwavering commitment to their vision. One story that stands out to me is the journey of Fifth & Cor. This transformation was only possible because of a commitment to my vision, an openness to adapt, and a strong belief in the power of creative marketing.

To cultivate resilience and adaptability in pursuit of your vision, it's essential to develop a mindset that views challenges as stepping stones, not roadblocks. Set meaningful goals, embrace creativity, and surround yourself with a supportive community. The most successful leaders are those who adapt to change, stay focused on their purpose, and maintain a positive, forward-thinking mindset. In the end, it's not about avoiding failure or setbacks but about staying true to your vision and adapting when necessary.

As you continue on your journey, remember that resilience is not just a trait, but a practice—and one that will propel you to new heights as you turn your vision into reality.

CONNECT WITH ROBIN

www.linkedin.com/in/robin-dimond
www.fifthandcor.com
www.instagram.com/fifthandcor
www.linkedin.com/company/fifth-and-cor
www.x.com/FifthandCor
www.pinterest.com/fifthandcor
www.youtube.com/@Fifth-and-Cor

"Nate and his wife run a very customer-friendly business. When they say, 'Where Service is More than a Transaction,' they really mean it."

"All services they offered are all beyond my expectations."

Tree Removal
Tree Trimming
& More!

218-831-1145

Nate's Property
MAINTENANCE

BRAINERD LAKES
Chamber of Commerce

Initiative
FOUNDATION

's Property
TENANCE
218-831-1145

Lakes
PROUD
SHOP. BUY. SUPPORT.

Photographer Credit: Heidi Schimnich

NATE MAENDEL "THE TREE SURGEON"

With over 30 years of expertise, we specialize in tree removal, trimming, and total property transformations. Year-round tree work, free estimates, and a passion for serving our community make us your go-to for a beautiful, safe outdoor space.

CALL NATE AND OUR NPM TEAM TO THE RESCUE!

218 - 831 - 1142
218 - 831 - 1145

Nate's Property
MAINTENANCE LLC

WHERE SERVICE IS MORE THAN A TRANSACTION

STRATEGIES FOR SETTING AND ACHIEVING TRANSFORMATIONAL CAREER GOALS IN 2025

by Teresa Saputo-Crerend, LaunchBreak Co-Founder

Having a vision is easy. Believing in that vision is trickier. Ideally, you will always believe in yourself. However, it's normal to have mixed feelings about that. Listen to your positive thoughts and to people in your life who, from a purely unselfish perspective, want to see you succeed. It was after a walk with an old friend that gave me that final push to start LaunchBreak.

The best lesson I learned at Columbia Business School is when it comes to good decision-making, ignore sunk costs. Just because you have invested effort, resources and personal capital into your career doesn't mean you can't change it. Pouring energy into something that doesn't work for you will not make the outcome better.

I was at a crossroads in my life. I knew one path would be comfortable, predictable and maybe even more responsible. There are absolutely times in life when you need to take that safer path. And there are times, no matter one's circumstances, when you need to take the risk.

Given our experience mentoring young adults, my co-founder, Philippa Portnoy and I boldly created something out of nothing. We talked to many people about the idea of creating a networking platform for women athletes. Some loved it. Some seemed bored but nodded in agreement anyway. Some told us that we are "civilians" in a tech world and ended the call. Unperturbed, we persisted. Soon enough we found 1,600 plus people interested in being a part of it!

Our LaunchBreak members are all inspiring. To get to the first level of collegiate sports is often a culmination of a busy and disciplined childhood. It's not easy.

There are some members that bring even more color to their bold and inspiring journeys. As a nine-year-old, one member played tackle football with the boys as there were no girls' leagues. She was one of the fastest and a leading scorer. As she got older she used that same energy when she confronted lawmakers about Title IX.

While on a community outreach trip to Kenya, another member (who played collegiate women's ice hockey) recognized that the local women wanted to play soccer to stay healthy but didn't have the resources to do it. This LaunchBreaker sent a cold email to one of the greatest women soccer players in the world asking for money to get a program started. It worked.

My advice? Recognize when you do your clearest thinking. Is it after exercise? Is it in the shower? Is it in the middle of the night (if so have a notepad nearby). Allocate goal-setting for those times. I work out certain challenges with LaunchBreak on my runs and schedule that into my week. Don't let negative thinking get in the way of listing your goals. Just getting them down on paper is a big step towards manifestation.

Don't discount any of your life experiences as they may all be preparing you for your ultimate career stop. Athletes who spent years training for their sport may wonder why they did it if only to pivot to a new career. From time to time, catalogue the soft and hard skills acquired along the way. You will be surprised how many may be relevant!

Recognize who doesn't believe in you and resist the urge to confront them as you prove them wrong. If they must have a lane in your life, make sure it's not yours as there is room on the track for many. Trust me, they will always be behind you.

Snap decisions will be necessary; simply trust your instincts and experience. This can be hard especially when you may be learning as you go which is often the case for founders. Recognize that accomplishing your goals will be the compilation of many decisions, including the good and the bad ones. Competing in tennis often meant losing points, games and even sets but still winning the match. I try to remember this.

CONNECT WITH TERESA

www.launchbreak.com

HOW TO CREATE A BOLD VISION FOR STARTING YOUR BUSINESS IN 2025

by Terra Winston and Marilyn Johnson of The SoloCEOs

A bold vision starts with a simple question: *"What is the change that I want to help create?"* Does the world need more inspiration? Does your town need more artisanal pies? Can your professional services help companies thrive? Big or small, getting clear on your impact gives you a foundation for building a vision. Once you have decided on your intended impact, next define HOW you will deliver it. For example, a communication consultant may set a vision to significantly increase their number of clients. Or they may decide to deepen their work with existing clients. Or they could turn their methodology into an online course to reach even more people. By starting with impact, you can then choose the most enjoyable and aligned version of your vision.

The SoloCEOs is the perfect example of a bold idea made real. We (Marilyn and Terra) would meet to share ideas and collaborate on projects. Over many cups of tea, we shared frustrations that there were few targeted resources for us - solo entrepreneurs with serious and viable businesses. Many of the podcasts, conferences, and courses we found were created assuming that every entrepreneur wants to grow into a huge corporation. Our bold idea was that solo businesses are not a temporary solution - they're a growing and important form of enterprise that has unique characteristics and deserves its own tools and communities. So we created it! We kicked off The SoloCEOs in 2019 with an in-person Summit and we've been going strong ever since.

For solopreneurs, it can be tempting to recreate goal setting the way it's done in big corporations by focusing only on growing revenue. Instead, start by revisiting your personal definition of success. Do you need a certain level of wealth or income? What about the quality of your life? Do you want to make a certain impact on your clients or the world? Once you define success, you can create meaningful goals that close the gap between the current state of your business and life and where you dream to be. At that point, use your strengths to build a solid plan for achieving those goals. Taking these aligned actions will give you the opportunity to manifest your dreams in the short and long-term.

In 2008, a stressed and frustrated Terra quit her day job with nothing more than a mortgage and a plan to rest and reset. After three months of exploring Argentina, she launched her business with only a simple business card from Kinko's. Her initial goal was modest—maintaining a minimum bank balance—but she has since built a thriving, impactful enterprise she truly loves. In contrast, Marilyn, tired of repeated layoffs, began her journey in 2001 by taking on small projects while defining her next professional steps. Over 23 years later and a steep learning curve, Marilyn developed a niche that blends her passion for helping others, her professional experience, and her education, creating a fulfilling and successful path of her own.

The most powerful and practical tool that you can find is community. Start connecting with fellow entrepreneurs who are willing to be vulnerable and transparent about the joys and challenges that they have faced. It's an amazing way to share resources, gain new perspectives, and be thought partners.

Before we started The SoloCEOs, we used to meet regularly to cheer each other on and problem-solve. We even had annual strategic reviews to get fresh thinking on our business plans. If you don't already have a strong circle of solopreneurs in your life, let us be part of your community! Our live-streamed Guru Talks and The SoloCEOs podcast can be an easy way to get started.

CONNECT WITH TERRA & MARILYN

www.soloceosummit.com
www.soloceosummit.com/home-page-2/talks
www.soloceosummit.com/home-page-2/the-podcast
www.instagram.com/soloceosummit

THRIVE TRANSFORM

ELEVATE YOUR LIFE !

Life Coach
Your Life, Your Blueprint!

PATHFINDING
Navigate Career Moves and Personal transitions

DECODING THE SIGNS
Understand Fatigue, Anxiety & Relationship Dynamics

BEYOND THE 9-5
Unleash your Potential, Create a Meaningful & Purposeful Life

TRANSFORMATION
Mater tools for Professional & Personal Growth

EMPOWER YOUR JOURNEY

First 10 "She Rises,"members receive 10% of Packages. Book FREE 45 min call TODAY!

WHY ME?

As a single parent, a professional, & someone who's walked through transitions & challenges, I bring not just expertise but real-life experience to the table. Customized Package; using Somatic techniques; MINDFULNESS, BREATHING, VISUALIZATION; I will help you gain Clarity, Find Purpose & bring Changes in your LIFE!

Stop Surviving, & Start Thriving!!!

transformthrive853@gmail.com

LEADERSHIP LESSONS FOR BUILDING A FUTURE-FOCUSED BUSINESS

by Winifred Ndukwe

The workplace of 2025 will look very different from what we've known. Rapid advancements in technology, shifting employee expectations, and global uncertainties mean one thing: businesses that embrace innovation, adaptability, and self-leadership at every level will win.

Here's how to cultivate a mindset and strategy that position your business and career for long-term success through leveraging artificial intelligence, leaning into change, setting a clear long-term vision, and empowering your people to lead from wherever they are.

1. Use Artificial Intelligence to Work Smarter, Not Harder

AI isn't just a trend—it's a game-changer. To get the most out of it, you need to move beyond treating it as a fancy tool and fully integrate it into your strategy.

- **Smarter decision-making**: AI helps you predict trends, spot risks, and uncover opportunities faster than any manual process.
- **Driving innovation**: By automating repetitive tasks, AI gives your team more time to focus on creativity and solving complex problems.
- **AI security**: Cyber threats are real. Don't adopt AI without a plan to secure your systems and protect sensitive data.

The businesses that treat AI as an enabler, not just a shortcut, will be the ones driving smarter decisions and faster innovation.

2. Turn Change Into Growth

Change isn't the enemy—it's the catalyst for growth. In 2025, businesses that thrive will be those that see change as a chance to improve, rather than something to endure.

- **Foster agility**: Create a culture where your team feels comfortable experimenting and learning from failure.
- **Upskill your people**: Invest in training and resources to help employees adapt to new tools and trends.
- **Challenge assumptions**: The strategies that worked yesterday might hold you back tomorrow. Be ready to pivot.

When you approach change with curiosity rather than resistance, it opens the door to new opportunities.

3. Think Beyond the Next Quarter

Short-term wins are great, but they can't come at the expense of long-term growth. Building a resilient, future-focused business means planning for tomorrow, not just today.

- **Scenario planning**: Prepare for a range of outcomes, from the best-case scenario to the challenges you'd rather not think about.
- **Vision with flexibility**: Stay focused on your goals, but be ready to adapt your path as the landscape shifts.
- **Collaborative vision-building**: Bring your team into the process. A shared vision creates alignment and ownership.

Long-term success isn't about guessing what's ahead—it's about staying focused and adaptable, no matter what the future holds.

4. Empower Leadership at Every Level

Leadership isn't reserved for the corner office. In a future-focused business, everyone has a role to play in driving success, and empowering self-leadership is how you unlock that potential.

- **Delegate responsibility**: Give people the tools and freedom to lead in their roles. Trust is a powerful motivator.
- **Celebrate contributions**: Acknowledge efforts at every level. Recognition fuels confidence and inspires others to step up.
- **Build skills**: Leadership can be taught. Encourage continuous learning and offer opportunities for growth.

When everyone feels ownership of their work, the entire organization becomes more resilient, innovative, and adaptable.

The Future Is Yours to Shape

2025 will be defined by bold ideas, strong leadership, and businesses that aren't afraid to embrace the unknown. It's a year for thinking big, taking calculated risks, and empowering your people to rise to the challenge.

Whether it's leveraging AI, turning change into growth, or fostering leadership at all levels, the steps you take today will define your success tomorrow.

Winifred Ndukwe
Regional Cybersecurity Leader & Founder, The Corporate Leader Blueprint

FAITH, FOCUS, AND PURPOSE: CHRISTINE DAVIS'S JOURNEY TO EMPOWERING WOMEN

In the hustle and bustle of everyday life, it's easy to lose sight of our dreams. Responsibilities, setbacks, and moments of uncertainty can make us question whether our goals are even attainable. Yet, countless women have shown perseverance, faith, and focus can make dreams a reality. Among these women is Christine Davis, founder of Anointed Assistant, who exemplifies the power of determination and purpose.

Christine's journey began with a vision: to create a company that empowered small businesses to thrive and allowed her the flexibility to prioritize her family. As a wife and mother, Christine understood the importance of being present for her loved ones. Yet, she also felt a deep calling to use her talents to help others. That balance between professional ambition and personal fulfillment became the foundation of Anointed Assistant.

Starting a business is rarely straightforward. Christine faced her share of challenges, including moments of profound loss and uncertainty. But through it all, she leaned on her faith. *"Seeing the end before the beginning means walking in faith."* This mindset helped her stay focused on her purpose, even when the journey seemed unclear. By trusting God's plan and relying on His guidance, she found the strength to push through the obstacles.

Anointed Assistant was born out of a desire to help others succeed. Christine recognized that many small business owners struggle to manage their companies' day-to-day demands. Christine's company provides the tools and expertise businesses need to grow, from social media management to administrative support. By taking on these tasks, Anointed Assistant allows entrepreneurs to focus on their passions and priorities. Christine's work uplifts others and creates a ripple effect of growth and success in her community.

But Christine's story is about more than business success. It's about resilience and faith in the face of adversity. Like many women, she has experienced moments of heartbreak and loss that could have derailed her dreams. Instead of giving up, Christine chose to see these moments as opportunities for growth. She found blessings in unexpected places and learned to trust that God's timing is perfect.

One key to Christine's success has been her ability to stay focused on what God created her to be rather than conforming to the world's expectations. Today, it's easy to get caught up in comparison and self-doubt. Christine's advice to women is simple yet profound: *"Stay true to the purpose God has placed in your heart. Don't let the world's noise distract you from your calling."*

Her story is a testament to the power of faith, hard work, and perseverance. For women who feel like giving up, Christine's journey reminds them that setbacks are not the end of the story. Every challenge is an opportunity to grow stronger and move closer to your dreams. By focusing on the goal and trusting in God's plan, you can achieve more than you ever imagined.

As Christine reflects on her journey, she is filled with gratitude. Anointed Assistant has allowed her to fulfill her professional goals and has given her the freedom to spend quality time with her family. *"I never imagined I could have both,"* she says. *"But God's blessings are beyond what we can comprehend."*

For women who are chasing their dreams, Christine's story is a source of inspiration. It's a reminder that the path to success is rarely easy, but it's always worth it. Remember that your journey has a purpose. Trust in God, stay focused on your calling and keep pushing forward.

CONNECT WITH CHRISTINE

www.AnointedAssistant.com
www.facebook.com/AnointedAssistant
www.linkedin.com/in/anointedassistant

BLOOD MANSION

Robert Howell

www.storywriter.ca

As the body count rises, the question becomes how many will walk out of Blood Mansion.

Imagine Stephen King's ROSE RED built by H. H. HOLMES: and you get Blood Mansion. With 100 victims claimed, two paranormal teams and the one person who has seen all its victims try to put a stop to it. But who will survive?

Available in paperback and eBook. Amazon and Barnes & Noble.

Sample Review

This book was incredible! I was seriously hooked from the beginning. It's not your typical ghost story, it's so much more. I plan on reading this again in the near future because it was THAT good. And the ending...perfection. I really can't wait to see what else Robert Howell comes out with next!

For more reviews visit my website

Watch for:

Coming to SRS Publishing in 2025:
Blood Castle – sequel to Blood Mansion expected in March
A Devil of a Time – Urban Fantasy
Teen/Young Adult – Urban fantasy:
Charm Trilogy
Third Times The Charm: book one
The Fourth Charm: book two of
The Charms Together: book three
Release dates to be posted to my website.
More to come!

About Myself

A native Montrealer I have done much travelling, and this is reflected in my writing. Every place I visit gives me more ideas that I weave into my storytelling.

My life experiences also feature in my writing, from college to the military and my years working in multiple aspects of the real estate industry.

I write in various genres both in my novels and short stories.

I am a father of four and grandfather of three.

A full-author biography is on my website.

BEAUTIFUL BURNED BRIDGE

by Teri Katzenberger

We've all heard the saying, *"Be careful not to burn bridges."* It's usually framed as a cautionary warning: *"You don't want to burn any bridges!"*

The phrase originated from the literal act of destroying a bridge or path behind you, ensuring that no one could follow. Over time, it's come to symbolize intentionally cutting off relationships, opportunities, or connections. Burning bridges is often seen as a last resort, something reckless or irrevocable, leaving no chance for return.

But here's the question I keep asking myself: *"Is it really that bad to burn a bridge?"* I mean, let's be honest—we need to guard ourselves against people who aren't truly for us. If someone isn't for you, then by default, they're against you. That doesn't mean they're outwardly hostile, but it does mean they don't contribute positively to your life. People cannot love you and hate you at the same time. That's not how this realm works.

I ask myself again: *"To burn or not to burn the bridge?"*
It's a big question. One worth exploring. Because maybe, just maybe, burning a bridge isn't always a loss. Sometimes, it's the first step toward building a better one.

Vengeance isn't necessary. I don't believe in karma—I walk in faith and trust in God. I focus on being who He created me to be. We don't have to be on the attack. Let others burn their own paths of hatred and discontent; you don't have to join them.

It's easier to follow the crowd than to chart your own course and live by your Personal Life Standards. Many people don't want to see others succeed or live joyfully—misery loves company. I refuse to hang out with misery. The smaller my circle, the more peace I have.

Words of Wisdom: Don't rebuild the bridges others have burned. If they don't love you, or support you, let the ashes lay. It's natural to want everyone to like us, but you don't need to chase toxic relationships. Trust me—don't waste your energy on bridges that lead back to haters, bullies, or pot stirrers.

I spent years crossing bridges to people who didn't deserve my time. I've had to forgive myself for letting their actions steal so much of my life. But now, I see that my true bridge—the one I'm building—is beautiful and leads to peace and purpose.

The truth is, when we stop crossing back to toxic people, they accuse us of burning bridges. But we aren't responsible for their paths. We're responsible for our own mental and emotional wellness.

So, keep moving forward. Let the haters hate. You have nothing to lose, nothing to prove, and everything to gain by living boldly on your own beautiful bridge. There are dream stealers in our midst. I challenge you to become a Dream Releaser! Join me in fanning your flames to spark the fire within your spirit. Setting your Soul on fire! You deserve to be set free!

I would be honored to connect with you. I help women overcome hurts, habits and hang ups that continue to hold them back from achieving their best happy, healthy self and fulfilled life. You are welcome to reach out anytime. I would love to have a virtual coffee talk with you!

With Deep Love,
Teri Katzenberger
Founder - Owner
Live Well Now Academy LLC
terikatzenberger@msn.com
Functional Health and Lifestyle Wellness Specialist
#1 International Best-Selling Author

CONNECT WITH TERI

www.livewellnow.academy
www.terikatzenberger.onlineworkoutclub.com
www.facebook.com/TeriKatzenberger
www.instagram.com/terikatzenberger

NICE GIRLS FINISH FIRST: THE POWER OF AUTHENTIC LEADERSHIP

by Corinne Brown

The phrase *"Nice girls finish last"* is an outdated adage rooted in the belief that kindness, compassion, and authenticity are weaknesses in competitive environments. Yet, as societal dynamics shift and workplaces evolve, it's becoming increasingly clear that *"nice girls"*, women who lead with empathy, integrity, and collaboration, not only finish first but are reshaping leadership itself.

Authentic leadership is no longer a buzzword, it's a necessity. In an era where trust and connection are critical to success, the ability to lead with heart, clarity, and a sense of purpose sets effective leaders apart. Nice girls, the women who embrace these traits, are breaking through barriers, thriving in challenging environments, and proving that being nice is not synonymous with being weak.

Redefining Strength in Leadership

Strength is often equated with assertiveness, decisiveness, and an unyielding demeanour. While these traits have their place, they often leave no room for collaboration, listening, or vulnerability, all hallmarks of the *"nice girl."* These women lead differently. They build trust by genuinely listening to their teams, build resilience by empowering others, and create environments where people feel valued.

Studies show that employees are more engaged and productive under leaders who demonstrate emotional intelligence, a cornerstone of authentic leadership. Empathy and compassion are not liabilities, they're assets that drive loyalty and innovation. The *"nice girl"* succeeds because she leads from a place of understanding and connection, not domination.

Nice Doesn't Mean Complacent

Let's clear up one misconception, being nice doesn't mean avoiding difficult conversations or shying away from tough decisions. Authentic leaders set boundaries, hold others accountable, and stay true to their values. The difference lies in how they approach these challenges. They deliver feedback constructively, manage conflicts with diplomacy, and make decisions that reflect both strength and empathy.

Why Nice Girls Are Thriving

The world is embracing change. Diversity and inclusion are no longer optional, and the top-down, authoritarian leadership style of the past is giving way to more inclusive, people-centered approaches. Nice girls are perfectly positioned to thrive in this landscape. Their ability to lead with authenticity resonates with modern workplaces that value collaboration over competition and people over profits.

Moreover, leading with kindness cultivates psychological safety, a critical factor for innovation and growth. When people feel safe to share ideas, take risks, and admit mistakes, organisations thrive.

Practical Strategies for Leading as a *"Nice Girl"*
1. Embrace Your Authenticity
Stop apologising for being kind and compassionate. These qualities set you apart in a world that desperately needs them. Trust that leading with integrity will inspire others to follow suit.

2. Set Boundaries
Kindness doesn't mean saying yes to everything. Learn to set clear boundaries and prioritise your well-being. By respecting yourself, you teach others to respect you.

3. Communicate Assertively
Speak up with confidence and clarity. Nice girls can deliver powerful messages without losing their warmth. Assertiveness is not the opposite of kindness, it's a complement to it.

4. Lead by Example
Show others that success doesn't require stepping on others. Demonstrate how collaboration, empathy, and mutual respect lead to better outcomes.

5. Celebrate Wins
Recognise and celebrate your team's achievements. Kindness breeds loyalty, and loyalty fuels success.

In the End:
Nice girls finish first not because they compromise, but because they excel. Their ability to lead authentically, inspire trust, and work in collaboration is transforming workplaces and shattering stereotypes. In a world that often undervalues kindness, these women prove that it's the secret ingredient to lasting success.

CONNECT WITH CORINNE

corinnebrowncoaching@gmail.com
www.corinnebrowncoaching.com
www.instagram.com/corinnebrowncoaching
www.facebook.com/Corinne Brown Coaching
www.linkedin.com/in/corinne-brown-36513673

The SHE RISES STUDIOS PODCAST

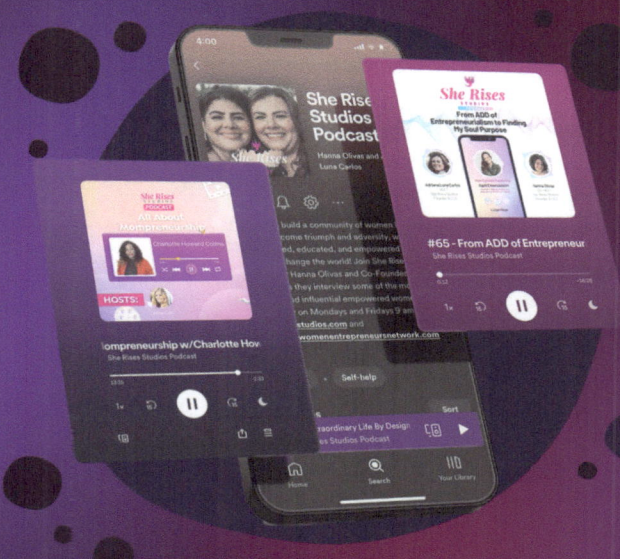

The She Rises Studios podcast is dedicated to empowering women like you to reach their full potential and live their best lives. With inspiring stories, insightful interviews, and practical advice from experts in different industries, our podcast is your go-to source for information, inspiration, and motivation. Join us as we explore topics like:

- Overcoming self-doubt and limiting beliefs
- Building and running a successful business
- Building confidence and Self-esteem
- Navigating career transitions
- Starting and growing a business
- Balancing work and family life
- Improving physical and mental health
- Finding meaning and purpose in life
- So many more

Our guests include successful entrepreneurs, inspiring thought leaders, and everyday women who have overcome challenges and achieved their dreams. Each episode is packed with actionable tips and strategies to help you take your life to the next level.

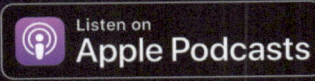

IGNITE YOUR NEW YEAR: SETTING BOLD INTENTIONS FOR AN EMPOWERED LIFE

by Michele Bischof

As the clock strikes midnight and 2025 begins, an undeniable energy fills the air—a promise of fresh starts and new possibilities. Yet, how often have we set New Year's resolutions only to feel disconnected from them by February? I've been there. Years ago, after a severe back injury from a car accident, I was stuck in frustration and overwhelm, unsure if I could reclaim my health, confidence, or purpose. What I discovered during that challenging time is now the foundation of what I teach women worldwide: transformation doesn't come from resolutions—it comes from intention.

A New Year, A New Way

Hi, I'm Michele Bischof, a Holistic Health and Fitness Coach and 2x Best-Selling Author. My mission is to empower women to step into their most vibrant, confident, and fiery selves. Through my Empowered Life Principles and signature Ignite Method, I've helped women break free from limiting beliefs, reconnect with their inner power, and take bold action toward the lives they desire. The power to change your life isn't out there—it's already within you. You just need the tools to uncover it.

Why Intentions Ignite Transformation

Unlike resolutions, which focus on external outcomes, intentions are rooted in how you want to feel. They align your actions with your values. For example:

- A resolution might be: *"I'll go to the gym five days a week."*
- An intention could be: *"I will honor my body by moving it in ways that feel joyful and strong."*

Feel the difference? Intentions empower you to align your actions with the woman you're becoming. This year, try my Ignite Method to set bold, meaningful intentions.

The Ignite Method: Your Path to Transformation

1. Ignite Awareness

Before setting goals, reflect. Ask yourself:

- What do I want to feel in 2025?
- What's holding me back from stepping into my power?
- What lights me up and makes me feel alive?

Spend 10 minutes journaling your answers. Awareness is the first step—it's like flipping on the light in a dark room.

2. Ignite Intention

Choose one guiding word for the year—perhaps strong, vibrant, or bold. Let this word shape how you show up each day. Then write 1–3 intentions that align with it.

If your word is strong:

- *"I will fuel my body with nourishing foods."*
- *"I will lift weights twice a week to build strength."*
- *"I will say no to things that drain my energy."*

3. Ignite Action

Intentions come to life through consistent action. Start small. What can you do today to feel closer to your desired outcome?

Try this:

- Create a vision board with images that reflect your guiding word.
- Set a 7-day micro-goal, like drinking more water or meditating for 5 minutes daily.
- Celebrate small wins—progress fuels momentum.

Your Year of Empowerment Starts Now

This year, release perfection and embrace the power of intention. You don't need to have it all figured out or wait until you feel *"ready."* The most important thing is to start.

2025 is your year to rise, ignite your fire, and boldly step into the woman you're meant to be. What's your guiding word? Write it down, say it out loud, and take one small action today to bring it to life.

You've got this—and I'm cheering you on every step of the way.

PS: Bold intentions are powerful, but bold action is where the magic happens. Ready to ignite your fire and transform your life in 2025?

☀ **Book your FREE Igniter Discovery Session** today and take the first step toward vibrant health and unstoppable energy. 👉 **Book Now**

Don't miss my **Fierce and Fabulous 10 Ways to Thrive Guide**—packed with strategies to fuel your transformation. 🔥 **Download Here**

BECOMING UNSTOPPABLE: THE ART OF WEDDING PLANNING WITH GIRASOLE & CO. WEDDINGS

by Heather Arra

Planning a wedding can feel like navigating a beautiful maze, with every twist and turn representing a decision or dream. With nearly a decade of experience, I totally get the emotional rollercoaster couples ride on their journey to *"I do."* At Girasole & Co. Weddings in Columbus, OH, we aim to make this often-daunting process feel like an exciting adventure, letting couples focus on what really matters—their love.

Our Vision

When I moved from New Jersey to Ohio in 2022, I knew I wanted to start Girasole & Co. Weddings to blend artistry and elegance into unforgettable experiences. Every wedding should tell the couple's unique love story, and my goal is to help bring that vision to life with careful planning. I've always wanted to make a real difference during this joyful time, ensuring it's more about happiness and less about stress.

Balancing Life and Wedding Planning

One big challenge couples face is finding the balance between wedding planning and their everyday lives. Work, family, and social commitments can quickly become overwhelming. That's where we step in! Our client-centered approach means we handle all the details, so couples can focus on each other and what their big day means to them. We're here to help create celebrations that truly reflect their essence while taking away the stress.

Support is Key

In this industry, having a reliable support system is crucial. At Girasole & Co. Weddings, our Type A personalities ensure no detail slips through the cracks. We excel at multitasking and supporting our clients every step of the way—whether it's communicating with vendors or managing the timeline on the big day. I always remind my clients, *"Your wedding is a reflection of you,"* which drives our passion for personalized event design.

Giving Back to Mental Health

I'm proud to share that a core value of my business is making a difference beyond the wedding day. We donate a percentage of every booking to mental health support organizations. Mental well-being is so important, and I believe in giving back to the community while supporting those in need. Weddings can be stressful, and I want to ensure that while we're celebrating love, we're also promoting mental health awareness.

Finding Joy Amidst the Chaos

Weddings should be joyous occasions, but planning can sometimes overshadow that happiness. I always encourage couples to carve out moments of joy amid the chaos—whether it's a cozy date night to brainstorm ideas or chatting with family about their plans. Personally, I love unwinding with my dog, Sadie, and binge-watching uplifting shows like Sweet Magnolias and Virgin River. These little rituals remind me of the importance of self-care during busy times, and I hope my clients find their own ways to relax, too!

A Commitment to Excellence

At Girasole & Co. Weddings, our mission is to create a positive experience that uplifts couples. We understand how significant this day is and take our role seriously. Looking back at the couples I've worked with, I cherish the love stories that have unfolded and the connections that have deepened during the planning process.

Becoming Unstoppable

So, what have I learned on this journey as a wedding planner? Success lies in empowering couples to enjoy their love stories without the stress. At Girasole & Co. Weddings, we're all about turning wedding planning into an exhilarating adventure rather than a chore.

To all the brides and grooms out there: embrace the journey! With the right support and a clear vision, you can create a day that's truly memorable and reflects the unstoppable love you share. Let's embark on this beautiful adventure together, making your dream wedding a reality while also building a community that values mental well-being!

CONNECT WITH HEATHER

www.girasoleco.com
www.facebook.com/girasoleco
www.instagram.com/girasolecoweddings

SACRED TIMING:
A Journey into 2025

(OR HOW I FINALLY LEARNED TO STOP SPEED DATING MY PROJECTS)

There I was, arranging my medicine bundle under a full moon that looked suspiciously like a cosmic disco ball. "Universe, are you throwing a party or sending me a message?" 40+ years, still the spirits love to make me laugh at precisely the moments I'm trying to be all serious and shamanic.

My phone sparkled with notifications – another speaking request, three workshop inquiries, and probably a partridge in a pear tree. My default "yes" setting had been working overtime lately. You want a workshop? Yes! A book? Yes! An online program about teaching alpacas to meditate? Well... I probably said yes before they finished asking.

During my last vision quest (included an unexpected visit from a very opinionated squirrel), I received an image that made me laugh: a sacred cow lounging on a pile of unwritten stories, wearing reading glasses and marking manuscripts with a red pen. Message received, spirits – subtle as a mariachi band at a meditation retreat.

As my workshop space filled with beautiful souls, all carrying that familiar look of "I'm here for transformation but also slightly worried this might involve dancing." As they settled into the circle, I shared my recent revelation from a dream: "The shamans say we can call back missed opportunities, but first we have to clean house – it's like spiritual Marie Kondo!

Tonight is the last night of 2024 and we are creating our death arrows, I added my own ribbons and a feather from this morning. Each one represented a program or habit that had overstayed its welcome, like that house guest who keeps "finding" reasons to extend their stay.

"What story wants to emerge?" I asked, mentally adding, "And please don't let it be another '44 Steps to Something' program." The universe, with its impeccable comic timing, sent a gentle breeze that made all our papers dance.

A participant tearfully confessed her addiction to saying yes, I jumped "Oh honey, I once said yes so many times in one day, my spirit guides started sending me throat lozenges in my dreams."

That night, watching our death arrows in the fire, I witnessed my sacred cows doing their final tap dance in the flames. 40+ years collecting wisdom, and here was the plot twist:

Sometimes the most powerful medicine is in the spaces between the ceremonies, in the cosmic pause button, in the divine permission slip to just be.

2025 was beckoning with a different rhythm – less salsa marathon, more sacred swing dance. Instead of racing to fill every space in my calendar with

by Charel Morris

workshops, I'd blocked out entire weeks for what I'm calling 'Sacred Nothing' time for the universe to pencil in its own appointments. Not abandoning the work, but letting it breathe, transform, and occasionally crack jokes. Like those wise mountain folks sharing their last potatoes, I'm learning that true abundance includes a healthy portion of holy laughter.

As the fire whispered its last punchlines, I opened my journal. The story wasn't about the next big program or the next transformational hit. It was about dancing with the mysteries, surfing the sacred waves of change, and remembering that even the most profound spiritual truths come with a side of cosmic comedy.

That opinionated squirrel from my vision quest. Pretty sure I saw him nodding in approval from a nearby tree. Either that, or he was just judging my fire-tending skills. With spirit animals, you never really know.

 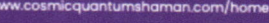

🌐 www.cosmicquantumshaman.com/home

in www.linkedin.com/in/charelmorris

 www.instagram.com/cybershaman

 www.facebook.com/charel.morris

🌐 https://www.cosmicquantumshaman.com/instant-zen

📅 https://www.cosmicquantumshaman.com/calendar

Sacred Timing: A Journey into 2025

by Charel Morris

"In just six months, Charel helped me transform my weekend retreats into a 42-day experience for women in community. Her expanded mindset will amaze you to see things you never imagined." -Kristina S., International Retreat Leader

"After a long day or week of work, my mind is tired, and I don't feel myself. Engaging with Charel and the women in my Circle of Power soothes my mental fatigue and invigorates how I approach each new week." -Melanie Ensign

Unlock Your Quantum Potential 40 years guiding thousands in unlocking their innate healing potential - from parents to multinational executives.

My approach combines ancient shamanic wisdom with cutting-edge energy medicine to help you:

- Access deeper creativity and insight
- Clear energetic blocks
- Align business with transformation
- Tap natural healing abilities
- Blend spiritual energy into life

"Charel's program teaches you tools to help ground yourself and cope with the stresses of the corporate world and everyday life. I love her spirit and energy!" - Kalika D., Corporate Executive

The Science Behind the Magic: My signature approach combines Scalar Wave, Quantum Realm techniques, and practical strategies for:

- Healing and Wellness
- Business Growth
- Leadership Development
- Personal Transformation

Global Experience:
- DEF CON Conventions (700 to 33,000+ attendees)
- International Security Conferences
- International Open Source Conferences
- Corporate Board Retreats
- Global Transformation Events

"The results speak for themselves! If you're struggling with an issue, I highly suggest working with Charel." -Diane B., Executive Career Coach

YOUR WORK WAS SURPRISING. I DISCOVERED HOW TO MOVE MY ENERGY OUT ALONG 'ENERGY FIBERS' TO MEET FUTURE CLIENTS! IT WAS FUN & ILLUMINATING." -TRAVIS ROSSER, ENTREPRENEUR & SPEAKER, CO-FOUNDER OF KAJABI

The Revolutionary Power of Scalar Wave Healing

My Personal Healing Journey: When traditional medicine failed my severely broken ankle, I turned to Scalar Wave Healing. The results? Complete healing in three weeks, with X-rays showing fully restored bone and realigned tissues - no surgery needed.

After a fall, my first doctor refused to cast my broken ankle. For 60 days, it healed incorrectly - severe calcification, displaced tendons, and bone fragments. A second doctor, facing potential surgery, provided proper casting but warned surgery might still be necessary if the tendons didn't realign.

Scalar Wave Benefits:
- Activates cellular-level healing
- Improves circulation
- Reduces inflammation
- Releases deep tension
- Zero side effects

"While her work struck me as 'magical,' it turned out to be immensely practical. The results speak for themselves!"
-Diane B., Executive Career Coach

Ready to Transform Your Life, Business, or Health? Book a Discovery Call | Learn About Scalar Wave Therapy

Let's Chat About Your Path

MARIANA ALVAREZ:
EMPOWERING FAMILY-OWNED BUSINESSES WITH FINANCIAL CLARITY, SUPPORTED BY A SPECTACULAR TEAM

by Mariana Alvarez

Mariana Alvarez, MSA, EA, is the founder and CEO of Controller Works, a fully virtual accounting firm that helps family-owned businesses achieve financial clarity and sustainable growth. With over 15 years of experience in accounting, Mariana has dedicated herself to providing clients with tools and strategies to build financial stability. Behind Controller Works' success is not only her leadership but also a talented team committed to delivering exceptional service.

A Vision Born from Resilience and Purpose
Raised in a family that valued education and entrepreneurship, Mariana developed an early appreciation for hard work and learning. However, her journey was marked by adversity, including leaving an abusive marriage and rebuilding her life as a single mother. These experiences inspired her to channel her resilience into creating Controller Works—a firm that supports others in overcoming challenges and achieving their goals.

"I understand what it's like to face financial uncertainty," Mariana shares, reflecting on her personal and professional challenges. This empathy, combined with her expertise, forms the foundation of Controller Works' mission: to provide businesses with not only financial clarity but also a trusted partner who cares about their success.

Values That Define Success
Controller Works is guided by core values of transparency, kindness, integrity, and gratitude. These principles inform every aspect of the firm's operations and client interactions. Mariana and her team emphasize open communication, ethical practices, and building long-term relationships based on trust and mutual respect.

Mariana's commitment to these values extends beyond her professional life. She openly shares her story to inspire others to overcome adversity, believe in second chances, and create lives of purpose and meaning.

A Stellar Team Driving Success
The heart of Controller Works lies in its team, which spans West Virginia, Florida, North Carolina, and Brazil. This diverse group of accountants and bookkeepers brings expertise, dedication, and a shared passion for helping clients succeed. *"Our team is the backbone of Controller Works,"* says Mariana. *"Their professionalism and kindness make all the difference for our clients."*

By fostering a positive work environment, Mariana ensures her team is motivated and equipped to go above and beyond.

This collaborative spirit allows Controller Works to deliver exceptional service while maintaining a personal touch.

Comprehensive Services for Financial Excellence
Controller Works offers a robust suite of services designed to meet the unique needs of family-owned businesses, with a focus on the construction industry. These services include:

- Bookkeeping and Accounting
- Expense Tracking and Budgeting
- Project Costing and Profitability Analysis
- Payroll and Compliance
- Financial Coaching and Strategy

With a team dedicated to excellence, these services are delivered with precision, collaboration, and a focus on empowering clients to regain control of their finances.

A Trusted Partner for Family-Owned Businesses
Controller Works is more than an accounting firm—it's a partner for family-owned businesses navigating financial complexities. Mariana's personal experiences enable her to connect with clients on a deeper level, while her team's expertise ensures tailored solutions for each unique challenge.

Building a Legacy Together
Mariana's journey and Controller Works' success are a testament to resilience, teamwork, and shared values. Together with her stellar team, Mariana is creating a legacy of empowerment, helping clients turn financial challenges into opportunities for growth.

For family-owned businesses seeking a partner who truly understands their needs, Controller Works offers a unique blend of expertise, empathy, and dedication. Through collaboration and personalized solutions, the team is helping clients achieve their financial goals and build a brighter future.

CONNECT WITH MARIANA
www.controllerworks.com
www.linkedin.com/in/mariana-alvarez-268269208
www.linkedin.com/company/94113647
www.facebook.com/profile.php?id=100091949612677